CARRYING THE DARKNESS
THE POETRY OF THE VIETNAM WAR

Edited by
W. D. Ehrhart

TEXAS TECH UNIVERSITY PRESS
1989

Cover and jacket design by Patricia Barrows Maines

Library of Congress Cataloging-in-Publication Data

Carrying the darknesss : the poetry of the Vietnam War / edited by W. D. Ehrhart.
    p.   cm.
    ISBN 0-89672-187-187-6 : $12.95 — ISBN 0-89672-188-4 (pbk.) : $6.95
    1. Vietnamese Conflict, 1961-1975—Poetry. 2. American poetry—20th century. 3. War poetry, American. I. Ehrhart, W. D. (William Daniel), 1948-
    PS595. V5C37   1989
    811'.54'080358—dc19   88-38691
                                                              CIP

Printed in the United States of America

Texas Tech University Press
Lubbock, Texas 79409-1037 USA

CREDITS

All poems appear by permission of the respective authors unless otherwise indicated.

Michael Anania: "A Second-Hand Elegy," *The Color of Dust,* Michael Anania, Swallow Press, 1970.

Philip Appleman: "Peace with Honor" and "Waiting for the Fire," *Open Doorways,* Philip Appleman, W. W. Norton Co. Inc., 1976.

John Balaban: "Graveyard at Bald Eagle Ridge" and "For Miss Tin in Hue" reprinted by permission of the publisher from *The Journal of General Education,* copyright © 1971–72 by The Pennsylvania State University Press. "The Guard at the Binh Thuy Bridge," "Mau Than," "Along the Mekong" and "The Dragonfish" reprinted from *After Our War,* copyright © 1974 by John Balaban, by permission of the University of Pittsburgh Press. "Thoughts Before Dawn" was in manuscript. All other poems reprinted from *Blue Mountain,* copyright © 1982 by John Balaban, by permission of Unicorn Press, Inc., P.O. Box 3307, Greensboro, NC 27402.

Jan Barry: "Green Hell, Green Death," "Floating Petals" and "Nights in Nha Trang," *Winning Hearts and Minds,* Jan Barry, Basil T. Paquet and Larry Rottmann, eds., 1st Casualty Press, 1972. "Harvest Moon," *Demilitarized Zones,* Jan Barry and W. D. Ehrhart, eds., East River Anthology, 1976. "In the Footsteps of Genghis Khan," *Veterans Day,* Jan Barry, Samisdat Press, 1982. "A Nun in Ninh Hoa" and "Lessons," *War Baby,* Jan Barry, Samisdat Press, 1983.

R. L. Barth: All poems reprinted from *Forced-Marching to the Styx,* R. L. Barth, Perivale Press, 1983.

Charles Fishman: "Death March" first appeared in *Samisdat* and was reprinted in *Mortal Companions*, Charles Fishman, Pleasure Dome Press, 1977.

Bryan Alec Floyd: All poems reprinted from *The Long War Dead*, Bryan Alec Floyd, The Permanent Press, 1983.

David Hall: "Disgrace" and "The Ambush of the Fourth Platoon," *Werewolf and Other Poems*, David Hall, Bald Mountain Press, 1981.

Gustav Hasford: "Bedtime Story," *Winning Hearts and Minds*, Jan Barry, Basil T. Paquet and Larry Rottmann, eds., 1st Casualty Press, 1972.

Steve Hassett: "Armed Forces Day" first appeared in *Rapport IV*, 2/1, 1973. "Mother's Day" first appeared in the *New York Quarterly Review*, #16, 1974. "Christmas" and *And what would you do, ma* first appeared in *Demilitarized Zones*, Jan Barry and W. D. Ehrhart, eds., East River Anthology, 1976. "Thanksgiving" and "Patriot's Day" were in manuscript.

Samuel Hazo: "Battle News," *Out of the War Shadow*, Denise Levertov, ed., 1968 War Resisters League Peace Calendar, 1967. Reprinted in *Once for the Last Bandit*, Samuel Hazo, University of Pittsburgh Press.

George Hitchcock: "Scattering Flowers" first appeared in *A Poetry Reading Against the Vietnam War*, Robert Bly and David Ray, eds., The Sixties Press, 1966.

Daniel Hoffman: "A Special Train," copyright © 1970 by Daniel Hoffman. Reprinted from *Broken Laws*, Daniel Hoffman, Oxford University Press, 1970.

Peter Hollenbeck: "Anorexia," copyright © 1984 by Peter Hollenbeck. Reprinted from *Three Views of Vietnam*, American Poetry and Literature Press, 1984.

John F. Howe: "The Land" first appeared in *Hair Trigger IV*, Columbia College (Chicago), 1980.

Christopher Howell: "Memories of Mess Duty and the War," *Why Shouldn't I,* Christopher Howell, L'Epervier Press, 1977. "A Reminder to the Current President" and "Liberty & Ten Years of Return," *Sea Change,* Christopher Howell, L'Epervier Press, 1985.

David Huddle: "Nerves" and "Cousin" first appeared in *The Little Review.* "Bac Ha" first appeared in *Southern Poetry Review.* "Theory," "Words" and "Vermont" first appeared in *Field.*

Allston James: "Honor (1969)," copyright © 1977 by Allston James. Reprinted from *The Mile Away Contessa,* Allston James, Angel Press, 1977.

Yusef Komunyakaa: "Somewhere Near Phu Bai" and "Starlight Scope Myopia" first appeared in *New England Review/Bread Loaf Quarterly.* "Tiger Lady" and "The Dead at Quang Tri" first appeared in *Writers Forum.* "Boat People" first appeared in *MSS.* "A Break from the Bush" and "After the Fall of Saigon" were in manuscript.

Herbert Krohn: "Farmer's Song at Can Tho" and "Ferryman's Song at Binh Minh" first appeared in *The New York Quarterly.* "Can Tho" first appeared in *Partisan Review.* "My Flute" first appeared in *The Nation.*

Lucy Lakides: "Armed Forces" was in manuscript.

James Laughlin: "The Kind-," copyright © 1978 by James Laughlin. Reprinted from *In Another Country,* James Laughlin, City Lights Books, 1978, by permission of the publisher.

McAvoy Layne: All poems are reprinted from *How Audie Murphy Died in Vietnam,* McAvoy Layne, Anchor Books, 1973.

Denise Levertov: Excerpts from "Staying Alive," *To Stay Alive,* copyright © 1971 by Denise Levertov Goodman. Reprinted by permission of New Directions Publishing Corporation.

Lou Lipsitz: "The Feeding," *Cold Water,* Lou Lipsitz, Wesleyan University Press, 1967.

Dick Lourie: "For All My Brothers and Sisters," *Anima*, Dick Lourie, Hanging Loose Press, 1979.

Paul Martin: "Watching the News" first appeared in *Nimrod*.

Gerald McCarthy: "The Hooded Legion" first appeared in *TriQuarterly* #59. All other poems reprinted from *War Story*, Gerald McCarthy, The Crossing Press, 1977.

Walter McDonald: "The Winter Before the War" first appeared in *Aura*, Winter 1979 (under the title "At Lake MacBride"). "Faraway Places" first appeared in *Ball State University Forum*, Autumn 1972. "For Kelly, Missing in Action" first appeared in *College English*, April 1973; reprinted by permission of the author and the National Council of Teachers of English. "Veteran" first appeared in *Re: Artes Liberales*, Fall 1978. "The Retired Pilot to Himself" first appeared in *South Dakota Review*, Spring 1974. "Hauling Over Wolf Creek Pass in Winter" first appeared in *TriQuarterly*, Winter 1984. "Caliban in Blue," "Faraway Places," "For Harper, Killed in Action," "For Kelly, Missing in Action," "Interview with a Guy Named Fawkes, U.S. Army," "Rocket Attack" and "The Retired Pilot to Himself" are reprinted from *Caliban in Blue*, Walter McDonald, Texas Tech Press, 1976. "Veteran" and "The Winter Before the War" are reprinted from *Burning the Fence*, Walter McDonald, Texas Tech Press, 1981. "War Games" and "Once You've Been to War" were in manuscript.

Thomas McGrath: "Reading the Names of the Vietnam War Dead," *The Movie at the End of the World*, Thomas McGrath, Swallow Press, 1972. "Go Ask the Dead," *Echoes Inside the Labyrinth*, Thomas McGrath, Thunder's Mouth Press, 1983.

Richard M. Mishler: "Ceremony" first appeared in *The Beloit Poetry Journal*, v.31, #4, Summer 1981.

Larry Moffi: "Putting an End to the War Stories," *A Simple Progression*, Larry Moffi, Ampersand Press, 1982.

James Moore: "One Reason I Went to Prison" first appeared in *Dacotah Territory,* and is reprinted from *The New Body,* James Moore, University of Pittsburgh Press, 1975.

David Mura: "The Natives" first appeared in *The American Poetry Review,* v.10, #1, January/February 1981. "Huy Nguyen: Brothers, Drowning Cries" first appeared in *Fallout,* Spring/Summer 1984.

Perry Oldham: "War Stories" first appeared in *Nexus,* Winter 1976. "Noon" was in manuscript.

Joel Oppenheimer: "Poem in Defense of Children," copyright © 1969 by Joel Oppenheimer. Reprinted from *In Time,* Joel Oppenheimer, The Bobbs-Merrill Co., Inc., 1969.

Simon J. Ortiz: "War Poem," *From the Belly of the Shark,* Walter Lowenfels, ed., Vintage Books, 1973.

Mark Osaki: "Amnesiac," *Breaking Silence: An Anthology of Contemporary Asian American Poets,* The Greenfield Review Press, 1983.

Basil T. Paquet: "Morning—A Death," "Group Shot" and "Mourning the Death, By Hemorrhage, of a Child from Honai" first appeared in *The New York Review of Books,* 18 December 1969. All others first appeared in *Winning Hearts and Minds,* Jan Barry, Basil T. Paquet and Larry Rottmann, eds., 1st Casualty Press, 1972.

Anthony Petrosky: "V.A. Hospital," *Jurgis Petrakas,* Anthony Petrosky, Louisiana State University Press, 1983. Reprinted by permission of the author and publisher.

John Clark Pratt: "Words and *Thoughts,*" copyright © 1974 by John Clark Pratt. Reprinted from *The Laotian Fragments,* John Clark Pratt, Avon Books, 1985.

Don Receveur: All poems reprinted from *Winning Hearts and Minds,* Jan Barry, Basil T. Paquet and Larry Rottmann, eds., 1st Casualty Press, 1972.

Dale Ritterbusch: "Search and Destroy" was in manuscript.

Larry Rottmann: "APO 96225," *Winning Hearts and Minds,* Jan Barry, Basil T. Paquet and Larry Rottmann, eds., 1st Casualty Press, 1972.

Vern Rutsala: "The Silence," *Laments,* Vern Rutsala, New Rivers Press, 1975.

John C. Schafer: "Battle Lines," *Demilitarized Zones,* Jan Barry and W. D. Ehrhart, eds., East River Anthology, 1976.

Richard Shelton: "Eden After Dark," *The Tattooed Desert,* Richard Shelton, University of Pittsburgh Press, 1971.

Joseph A. Soldati: "Surroundings," *Demilitarized Zones,* Jan Barry and W. D. Ehrhart, eds., East River Anthology, 1976.

William Stafford: "Report from an Unappointed Committee," copyright © 1985 by William Stafford. First appeared in *The Illiterati.* Reprinted from *Out of the War Shadow,* Denise Levertov, ed., 1968 War Resisters League Peace Calendar.

Michael Stephens: "After Asia" and "The Carp," copyright © 1985 by Michael Stephens.

Frank Stewart: "Black Winter," copyright © 1980 by Frank Stewart. First appeared in *The Paper* 1:1. Reprinted from *Peace Is Our Profession,* Jan Barry, ed., East River Anthology, 1981.

Bill Tremblay: "Mayday" and "Home Front," *Home Front,* Bill Tremblay, Lynx House Press, 1978.

Tom Wayman: "Despair," *Waiting for Wayman,* Tom Wayman, McClelland & Stewart Ltd., 1973. "Teething," *Living on the Ground,* Tom Wayman, McClelland & Stewart Ltd., 1980, by permission of the publisher.

Ron Weber: "A Concise History of the Vietnam War: 1965–1968" was in manuscript.

Bruce Weigl: "The Sharing" reprinted from *A Romance,* copyright © 1979 by Bruce Weigl, by permission of the University of Pittsburgh Press. "Anna Grasa" and "Monkey" first appeared in *Ironwood Magazine.* "Mines" and "Him, on the Bicycle" first appeared in *Field.* "Sailing to Bien Hoa" first appeared in *The Western Humanities Review.* "The Ambassador" reprinted from *Demilitarized Zones,* Jan Barry and W. D. Ehrhart, eds., East River Anthology, 1976. All other poems reprinted from *The Monkey Wars,* copyright © 1985 by Bruce Weigl, by permission of The University of Georgia Press.

Deborah Woodard: "Tower," copyright © 1984 by Deborah Woodard.

Ray A. Young Bear: "Wadasa Nakamoon, Vietnam Memorial" first appeared in *TriQuarterly #59.*

TABLE OF CONTENTS

xiv

CARRYING THE DARKNESS

CARRYING THE DARKNESS

Foreword to the 1989 Reprint

This corrected reprint edition of *Carrying the Darkness* incorporates a number of corrections to the original edition, including accurate texts for John Balaban's "The Dragonfish" and "For Mrs. Cam, Whose Name Means 'Printed Silk'" and for Walter McDonald's "For Kelly, Missing in Action."

Those who pay attention to small details will notice also that the subtitle of the anthology has been streamlined for this edition. I chose the original subtitle, *American Indochina—the Poetry of the Vietnam War*, in an attempt to convey the reality that what most Americans call the Vietnam War was actually a war that encompassed Cambodia and Laos as well. But a three-tiered title is just too cumbersome, and probably doesn't convey what I had hoped it would, so I've deleted "American Indochina."

I would like to dedicate this edition of the book to my daughter, Leela, in the fervent if futile hope that governments and nations might one day learn that armies are made of children, and that children are the only future we have.

W. D. Ehrhart
Philadelphia
September 1988

Foreword

. . . nobody
comes away in one piece.
D. F. Brown

When the Vietnam war began in 1946, most Americans were too busy celebrating the end of World War Two to notice a small brushfire war on the other side of the planet. Vietnam was known then—together with Cambodia and Laos—as French Indochina, and the war was a colonial war and a French problem. Many of the writers in this volume hadn't even been born yet. Nearly two decades would pass before American Marines would be deployed near Da Nang and the American people would come to realize just how near the other side of our planet can be. Still another agonized and agonizing decade would slowly drag by before the war in Southeast Asia would finally grind to a conclusion and Americans, weary and bruised, would begin to attempt to turn away at last from the most divisive episode in U.S. history since the War Between the States.

That attempt has been only partially successful at best. Throughout the later 1970s and into the 1980s, one issue after another has kept the memories alive: amnesty for draft resisters, Vietnamese refugees, POW/MIAs, Khmer Rouge genocide and the Vietnamese occupation of Cambodia, Agent Orange and growing U.S. involvement in Central America and the Caribbean. Simultaneously have come the questions: How did it happen? Who won and who lost? What might have been done differently? What did we learn and what should have been learned? Questions like these and a thousand others have been asked and answered in a thousand different ways in the decade since the war ended, and the debate will undoubtedly continue for decades to come.

But regardless of how one feels about the war—regardless of one's political perspective or personal point of view—there is little debate that Vietnam seared itself into the consciousness of virtually everyone who lived through those years, leaving no one unmarked.

That this is so will become readily apparent as you begin to read the poems in this anthology. Here are poems by combat soldiers and draft resisters, living-room observers and full-time activists, men and women, whites, blacks, Native Americans and Asian Americans, young and old and in between. Time may play tricks with human memory. Scholars and politicians, journalists and generals may argue, write and re-write "the facts." But when a poem is written, it becomes a singular entity with an inextinguishable and unalterable life of its own. It is a true reflection of the feelings and perceptions it records, and as such, it is as valuable a document as any history ever written. And the American experience in Indochina, whatever else it may have been responsible for, produced an outpouring of poetry unparalleled in American literature.

Far too much, in fact, to be included in any single anthology of manageable proportions. During the months I researched this book, I unearthed well over 5,000 poems, published and unpublished, written between 1961 and 1984. Even after I eliminated a great many poems for the simple reason that, however sincere they may have been, they just weren't very good poems, I was still faced with far more than I could include. Thus, I was faced with some very difficult decisions.

I chose, therefore, to offer as much space as possible to those younger poets who came of age during the Vietnam war and who are only now, if at all, beginning to establish themselves as writers—poets whose work, though not readily available, deserves a wider audience and greater recognition. Many of them, though not all, are Vietnam veterans. With the single exception of Michael Casey, author of *Obscenities* and winner of the Yale Younger Poets Series for 1972, who declined to have his poems included, I feel confident that what you will find here is a substantial portion of the best work by the best poets of the Vietnam generation.

In addition, I have tried to include at least enough poems by older writers to give one a sense of the depth and breadth of the poetry written by those already in their adulthood before the Marines landed. Of course, anyone at all conversant with contemporary American poetry, particularly poetry dealing with the Vietnam war, may be startled to find only a handful of poems by writers like Robert Bly and Denise Levertov—and none at all by the likes of Allen Ginsberg, Lawrence Ferlinghetti and David Ray. But I had to weigh the limited space I had against the fact that the work of most of these older poets is readily available from already existing sources.

I would also have liked to include translations of poetry by Vietnamese writers, but problems in acquiring an adequate and representational sampling of good translations to choose from, combined with the already overwhelming amount of material by Americans, finally led me to decide against it. Those interested in reading Vietnamese poetry in translation might begin with *Of Quiet Courage,* Jacqui Chagnon and Don Luce, eds., Indochina Mobile Education Project, 1974, John Balaban's *Ca Dao Viet Nam,* Unicorn Press, 1980, or one of the several collections of Thich Nhat Hanh also available from Unicorn Press.

Earlier anthologies of American poems dealing with Vietnam might also be of interest: *A Poetry Reading Against the Vietnam War,* Robert Bly and David Ray, eds., The Sixties Press, 1966; *Where Is Vietnam?,* Walter Lowenfels, ed., Anchor Books, 1967; *Out of the Shadow of War,* Denise Levertov, ed., War Resisters League 1968 Peace Calendar; *Winning Hearts and Minds: War Poems by Vietnam Veterans,* Jan Barry, Basil Paquet and Larry Rottmann, eds., 1st Casualty Press/McGraw Hill, 1972; *Listen: The War,* Tony Dater and Fred Kiley, eds., United States Air Force Academy Association of Graduates, 1973; *Demilitarized Zones: Veterans After Vietnam,* Jan Barry and W. D. Ehrhart, eds., East River Anthology, 1976; and *Peace Is Our Profession,* Jan Barry, ed., East River Anthology, 1981. All of these books are now out of print and difficult to obtain, but a diligent search among the stacks of a good library or used book store might yield results.

Lastly, I offer thanks to the many people without whose gracious patience and assistance this book would not have been possible:

To my wife, Anne Gulick Ehrhart, who supported me from the moment this project began until the moment it was finished, not only spiritually and emotionally—though she offered sustaining amounts of both—but also materially. She it was who assumed sole responsibility for earning a living while I stayed home day after day reading poetry and tinkering.

To the poets whose poems I have included, and in many cases to their publishers as well, for allowing me to reprint their work.

To the poets who made their work available to me, though I was unable to include them. Though I have no reservations about the poems I *have* included, I am equally certain that many of the poems I chose not to include deserve a better fate.

To Professor John Newman, Special Collections Librarian at Colorado State University, for giving me access to the many books and manuscripts in the library's Vietnam War Literature Collection.

To Professor Ralph J. Mills, Jr. of the University of Illinois at Chicago, Professor John Felstiner of Stanford University, Joseph Parisi of *Poetry*, Judith Neeld of *Stone Country*, Lee-lee Schlegal of *DEROS*, Joseph Bruchac of *The Greenfield Review*, Bob Seeley of *CCCO News Notes*, Mari LoNano of Associated Writing Programs, the staff of Poets & Writers Inc., Ken Lopez, Barry Sternlieb, Larry Heinemann, Gloria Emerson, and others I have undoubtedly forgotten to name, all of whom helped me to locate poets, poems and books.

To David A. Beck of G.C. Weimer Associates, Inc., for his generosity to a stranger.

To Jon Messick and his daughter, Briana, who helped to make a lonely but crucial week far from home bearable.

And finally to John Douglas, Senior Editor at Avon Books, who solved perhaps the knottiest dilemma I had to face. Numerous people whose judgement I respect urged me not to exclude my own work from this book, but for reasons I think quite obvious, I was loathe to decide otherwise—let alone to decide which poems or how many. John most kindly removed that burden from me, stepping in and serving as editor for my material, for which I am deeply grateful.

W. D. Ehrhart
Doylestown, Pennsylvania
January 1985

Glossary of Unfamiliar Terms

AK-47: automatic rifle used by the NVA and VC.
ao dai: traditional dress worn by Vietnamese women.
ARVN: Army of the Republic of Vietnam (South Vietnam); South Vietnamese soldier.
beaucoup: a lot.
beaucoup dien cai dau: roughly translated "very crazy," "insane."
berm: perimeter fortification, earthwork.
BOQ/PX: bachelor officers' quarters & post exchange.
butterfly: to be unfaithful.
C-4: plastic explosive.
chai: pidgin Thai for "true."
chogi stick: pole used for carrying baskets.
claymore: anti-personnel fragmentation mine.
CO: commanding officer or conscientious objector, depending on the context.
Cobra: helicopter gunship.
COC: command, operations & communications bunker.
cowboys: Saigon street toughs, often ARVN deserters or draft evaders.
CS: teargas.
dink: disparaging GI slang for a Viet Cong or any Vietnamese person.
dust-off: medical evacuation by helicopter.
F-105: jet fighter-bomber used by the U.S. Air Force.
F4 (F4C): jet fighter-bomber commonly called a "Phantom."
G-5: Civil Affairs; staff section of a military division responsible for relations with the civilian population.
gook: disparaging GI slang for a Viet Cong or any Vietnamese person.
greased: slang for killed.
hootch: house.
J: joint, marijuana cigarette.

liftship: helicopter.

L T (Lt.): lieutenant.

Mau Than: Year of the Monkey.

Mike Sixteen: M-16 automatic rifle.

MP: military police officer.

N'ai, N'ai chin: phonetic rendering of what the author recalls hearing attacking Vietcong soldiers shout; no translation possible.

nit-noy: pidgin Thai for "small."

NVA: North Vietnamese Army or North Vietnamese soldier.

O Club: officers' club.

O.D.: olive drab.

105: 105 millimeter artillery.

P: piaster; South Vietnamese money.

PR: personal recognizance.

punji stake: type of nonexplosive booby-trap.

Quad .50s: four .50 caliber machineguns, usually truck-mounted.

rach: river.

RTO: radio-telephone operator or radioman.

Saigon Tea: high-priced nonalcoholic drink served in bars catering to U.S. soldiers; when a GI bought a bargirl a drink, the bartender would serve the woman Saigon tea rather than alcohol.

sapper: demolitions expert.

short-time: about to rotate back to the U.S.

sin loi: roughly translated as "sorry about that."

slickship: helicopter troopship.

starlight scope: infra-red device for enhancing night vision.

Tchepone: town in southern Laos astride the Ho Chi Minh Trail.

tealoch: pidgin Thai for "second wife;" girlfriend or lover.

ti-ti: a little.

TOC: tactical operations center.

Trinh: Trinh Cong Son; popular Vietnamese folksinger of the 60s & 70s.

Udorn: airbase in Thailand used by the U.S. Air Force.

USARV: United States Army-Vietnam.

VC: Vietcong; also known as Victor Charlie or Charlie.

vill (ville): hamlet or village.
wadasa nakamoon: Mesquakie-Algonquin for "veteran's song."
Zippo: cigarette lighter.
zoomie: slang for pilot.

MICHAEL ANANIA

A Second-Hand Elegy

for Douglas Dickey, Pfc. U.S.M.C. *

"How can I be bitter?"
the fence-rows rolling with the land;
the last full measure of Ohio
measured by fence-rows compressing,
though parallel above receding hills,
the mixed hues of damp Spring greenery.

"I never knew him to be angry or afraid."
that is, assured of a providence
moving within the accidental turnings
of his life, he moved with certainty
among the farmyard's familiar disorders
and occasionally outward toward Dayton.

"He glanced for an instant at his friends—
    for only an instant—and then he jumped."
riding through Dayton on Saturday night
making the rounds, block by block,
the car radio marking time—
Downtown   Downtown—
the evening blush of neon blooming

into damp city air, the blue
clarity of mercury-lamp arcades;
four of them slouched in a Chevrolet
exhaust the evening, waiting for something to happen.

---

*In April of 1968 Douglas Dickey was awarded the Congressional Medal of Honor posthumously for throwing himself on a hand grenade during an engagement with the enemy in Viet Nam.

PHILIP APPLEMAN

Peace with Honor

Solitudinem faciunt,
pacem appellant.

1
The outer provinces are never secure:
our Legions hold the camps, their orders
do not embrace the minds
and hearts of barbarians. So, when the late-
late news reported the outlandish
screams in that distant temple,
the great bronze Victory toppled,
red stains in the sea, corpses
stranded by the ebb tide—all of that,
and only four hundred
armed men at the garrison—why,
of course it had to come, the massacre,
the plundering.

2
It was the decade's scandal at home,
the humiliation, the Eagles gone.
Senators put on grim faces
and gossiped over Bloody
Marys—what laureled head would roll for this?
Reports from the field
were cabled not to the Emperor but
to the Joint Chiefs, to filter
through at last, edited

and heavy with conclusions: the traitor,
they revealed, was not in uniform,
the treason was our own permissiveness;
in sterner times our Fathers would not
have suffered such dishonor.
We nodded: yes, they knew,
the Chiefs, what ancient virtue was.
The twilight shudders of matrons
seasoned our resolution. Somber, we took
a fourth martini, wandered to the couches,
the tables rich with peacocks' tongues,
and nodded,
nodded, waiting.

3

They sent our toughest
veterans, the Ninth Legion, the Fourteenth,
the Hundred-and-First, their orders un-
ambiguous: teach the barbarians respect.
Our marshals chose the spot: a steep defile
covering the rear, our regular troops drawn close,
light-armed auxiliaries at their flanks,
cavalry massed on the wings.
The enemy seethed everywhere, like a field
of wind-blown grasses.
There were the usual
harangues, the native leaders boasting
their vast numbers, screaming
freedom or death;
our generals, with that subtle sneer
they learn at the Academy,
pointing only to the Eagles on their tall shafts—
and every man remembered
the shame of Eagles fallen, comrades' bones
unburied: there was that curious thing,
men in bronze and steel, weeping.
And then the charge, the clash of arms,
cavalry with lances fixed, the glorious

victory: a hundred thousand tons of TNT
vaporized their villages, their forests were
defoliated, farmland poisoned forever,
the ditches full of screaming children,
target-practice for our infantry.
The land, once green and graceful,
running with pleasant streams in the rich brown earth,
was charred and gutted—not even a bird
would sing there again.

4

A glorious victory, of course,
but in a larger sense, a mandatory act
of justice: the general peace
was kept, the larger order held; peasants
for a thousand leagues around
are working their mules again.
Our prisoners and Eagles all returned,
we dine at the rich tables,
thinking of the Sunday games,
thinking of anything but rebellion—thinking
the honor of Empire
is saved.

Waiting for the Fire

Not just the temples, lifting
lotuses out of the tangled trees,
not the moon on cool canals,
the profound smell of the paddies,
evening fires in open doorways,
fish and rice the perfect end of wisdom;
but the small bones, the grace, the voices like
clay bells in the wind, all wasted.
If we ever thought of the wreckage

of our unnatural acts,
we would never sleep again
without dreaming a rain of fire:
somewhere God is bargaining for Sodom,
a few good men could save the city; but
in that dirty corner of the mind
we call the soul
the only wash that purifies is tears,
and after all our body counts,
our rape, our mutilations,
nobody here is crying; people who would weep
at the death of a dog
stroll these unburned streets dry-eyed.
But forgetfulness will never walk
with innocence; we save our faces
at the risk of our lives, needing
the wisdom of losses, the gift of despair,
or we could kill again.
Somewhere God is haggling over Sodom:
for the sake of ten good people
I will spare the land.
Where are those volunteers
to hold back the fire? Look:
when the moon rises over the sea,
no matter where you stand
the path of the light comes to you.

JOHN BALABAN

The Guard at the Binh Thuy Bridge

How still he stands as mists begin to move,
as morning, curling, billows creep across
his cooplike, concrete sentry perched mid-bridge
over mid-muddy river. Stares at bush-green banks
which bristle rifles, mortars, men—perhaps.
No convoys shake the timbers. No sound
but water slapping boatsides, banksides, pilings.
He's slung his carbine barrel down to keep
the boring dry, and two banana-clips instead of one
are taped to make, now, forty rounds instead
of twenty. Droplets bead from stock to sight;
they bulb, then strike his boot. He scrapes his heel,
and sees no boxbombs floating towards his bridge.
Anchored in red morning mist a narrow junk
rocks its weight. A woman kneels on deck
staring at lapping water. Wets her face.
Idly the thick Rach Binh Thuy slides by.
He aims. At her. Then drops his aim. Idly.

Along the Mekong

1. Crossing on the Mekong Ferry, Reading the August 14 *New Yorker*

Near mud-tide mangrove swamps, under the drilling
  sun

the glossy cover, styled green print, struck the eye:
trumpet-burst yellow blossoms, grapevine leaves,
—nasturtiums or pumpkin flowers? They twined
in tangles by our cottage in Pennsylvania.
Inside, another article by Thomas Whiteside.
2, 4, 5-T, teratogenicity in births;
South Vietnam 1/7th defoliated; residue
in rivers, foods, and mother's milk.
With a scientific turn of mind I can understand
that malformations in lab mice may not occur in
    children
but when, last week, I ushered hare-lipped, tusk-
    toothed kids
to surgery in Saigon, I wondered, what did they drink
that I have drunk. What dioxin, picloram, arsenic
have knitted in my cells, in my wife now carrying
our first child. Pigs were squealing in a truck.
Through the slats, I saw one lather the foam in its
    mouth.

2. River Market

Under the tattered umbrellas, piles of live eels
sliding in flat tin pans. Catfish flip for air.
Sunfish, gutted and gilled, cheek plates snipped.
Baskets of ginger roots, ginseng, and garlic cloves;
pails of shallots, chives, green citrons. Rice grain
in pyramids. Pig halves knotted with mushy fat.
Beef haunches hung from fist-size hooks. Sorcerers,
palmists, and, under a tarp: thick incense, candles.
Why, a reporter, or a cook, could write this poem
if he had learned dictation. But what if I said,
simply suggested, that all this blood fleck,
muscle rot, earth root and earth leaf, scraps
of glittery scales, fine white grains, fast talk,
gut grime, crab claws, bright light, sweetest smells
—Said: a human self; a mirror held up before.

3. Waiting for a Boat to Cross Back

Slouched on a bench under some shade,
I overhear that two men shot each other on the street,
and I watch turkey cocks drag cornstalk fans
like mad, rivaling kings in Kabuki
sweeping huge sleeve and brocaded train.
The drab hens huddle, beak to beak,
in queenly boredom of rhetoric and murder.
A mottled cur with a grease-paint grin
laps up fish scales and red, saw-toothed gills
gutted from panfish at the river's edge.

Mau Than

A Poem at Tet for To Lai Chanh

1

Friend, the Old Man that was last year
has had his teeth kicked in; in tears
he spat back blood and bone, and died.
Pielike, the moon has carved the skies
a year's worth to the eve. It is Tet
as I sit musing at your doorstep,
as the yellowed leaves scratch and clutter.
The garden you dug and plotted
before they drafted you, is now
stony, dry, and wanting a trowel.
"For my wife," you said, taking a plum,
but the day never came nor will it come
to bring your bride from Saigon.
Still the boats fetch stone, painted eyes on
their prows, plowing the banana-green river;
and neighbor children splash and shiver

where junks wait to unload their rock.
But shutters locked, the door of your house is locked.

2

A year it was of barbarities
each heaped on the other like stones
on a man stoned to death.
One counts the ears on the GI's belt.
Market meats come wrapped in wrappers
displaying Viet Cong disemboweled.
Cries come scattering like shot.
You heard them and I heard them.
The blessed unmaimed may have too.
So many go stumping about.
The night you left I turned off Hoa Binh
and saw a mined jeep, the charred family.
A Vietnamese cop minded the wreckage;
his gold buck teeth were shining
in a smile like a bright brass whistle.
Can you tell me how the Americans,
officers and men, on the night of
the mortaring, in the retching hospital,
could snap flash-photos of the girl whose
vagina was gouged out by mortar fragments?
One day we followed in a cortege
of mourners, among the mourners, slowly walking,
hearing the clop of the monk's knocking stick.

3

If there were peace, this river would be
a peaceful place. Here at your door
thoughts arrive like rainwater, dotting,
overspreading a dry, porous rock.
In a feathery drizzle, a man and wife
are fishing the river. The sidling waves
slap at her oar as she ladles the water
and fixes the boat with bored precision.
His taut wrists fling whirring weights;

the flying net swallows a circle of fish.
His ear wears a raindrop like a jewel.
Here at evening one might be as quiet
as the rain blowing faintly off
the eaves of a rice boat sliding home.
Coming to this evening
after a rain, I found a buff bird
perched in the silvery-green branches
of a water-shedding spruce. It was
perched like a peaceful thought. Then
I thought of the Book of Luke and, indeed,
of the nobleman who began a sojourn
to find a kingdom and return.

4

Out of the night, wounded
with the gibberings of dogs,
wheezing with the squeaks of rats,
out of the night, its belly split
by jet whine and mortar blast,
scissored by the claws of children,
street-sleepers, ripping their way free
from cocoons of mosquito netting
to flee the rupturing bursts
and the air dancing with razors
—out, I came, to safe haven.
Nor looked, nor asked further.
Who would? What more? I said.
I said: Feed and bathe me.
In Japan I climbed Mt. Hiei in midwinter.
The deer snuffled my mittens.
The monkeys came to beg.
I met Moses meeting God in the clouds.
The cold wind cleared my soul.
The mountain was hidden in mist. Friend,
I am back to gather the blood in a cup.

Graveyard at Bald Eagle Ridge

Solomon's Seal, False and True,
Jewel Weed and Arrowroot.
Here swallows, switching at bugs,
skirt the cornstalks' tassled tops
and skip above the sunken stones
of the hillside graveyard.
Farmers hold dearly to their dead;
their dead in childbirth, dead in war,
dead with sickness, dead with age.
Neatly as a kitchen garden,
they have tended the tombstones;
but, look, the woodchuck
burrows out a daughter's bones.
Will a tooth churn up? Cracked
wishbones of a child's hand?
Rainfogs lift up from the valley
which the dead are set to view.
Cowbells clang in earshot.
A white nag chomps the clover.
Looking out, the dead—the Shirks,
Browns, Gingerys, and Rines—
find their children green-haired,
socket-blind, and lying beside them.
In this year of our Lord,
a sparse generation tills the land.

Opening Le Ba Khon's Dictionary

So the Soul, that Drop, that Ray
of the clear Fountain of Eternal Day,
Could it within the humane flow'r be seen.
ANDREW MARVELL, "On A Drop of Dew"

The ink-specked sheets feel like cigar leaf;
its crackling spine flutters up a mildewed must.
Unlike the lacquered box which dry-warp detonated
—shattering pearled poet, moon, and willow pond—
the book survived, but begs us both go back
to the Bibliothèque in the Musée at the Jardin in
   Saigon,
where I would lean from ledges of high windows
to see the zoo's pond, isled with Chinese pavilion,
arched bridge where kids fed popcorn to gulping carp,
and shaded benches, where whores fanned their
   make-up,
at ease because a man who feeds the peacocks
can't be that much of a beast. A boatride,
a soda, a stroll through the flower beds.
On weekends the crowds could forget the war.
At night police tortured men in the bear pits,
one night a man held out the bag of his own guts,
which streamed and weighed in his open hands,
and offered them to a bear. Nearby, that night
the moon was caught in willows by the pond,
shone scattered in droplets on the flat lotus pads,
each bead bright like the dew in Marvell's rose.

The Dragonfish

Brown men shock the brown pools with nets.
Fishing for mudfish, carp and ca loc,
they step and stalk the banks; hurl;
stand, then squat heronlike in the
shadow-stretching, red evening dusk.

The pond is lovely where they fish,
one of many in a marshy field
linking delta paddies about Cao Lanh.
Phenol streaks, chartreuse and smoke blue,
curl, clot and twirl over the manila-bright,
sun-slanting surface, while silver chubs
flash after garbage scraps chugging out,
churning up, from an opening drain.

Five old tombs shadow the pond's far edge.
Their dripping stones are cut in characters
which no one, now, can read. Ghosts
of landlords click their tallies there.
Rain roils the water. Ducks dally
through twining blue morning-glory
trellising in spirals
over concertina barbed wire.
Like swallows or a weaver's shuttles,
darting jets, F-105s,
ply the curling fringes of the storm.

Rain spatters—wind scatters—
the water turned gun-barrel blue.
In sheeting rain, a wet dog grins
from a worn tomb's washing steps.
The dog snuffles a hen's feather.
It crackles old bones.

Far out in deserted paddies
more cratered than the moon,
guerrillas of the Front hide themselves
beneath slabs of rain-eaten tombs:
patient are they as lampwicks.

In squalling waters, North and South,
fishermen dredge, draw, dragnet up
a heavy fish, a dragon fish,
a land in the shape of the dragonfish.

For Miss Tin in Hue

The girl (captured; later, freed)
and I (cut by a centimeter of lead)
remember well the tea you steeped
for us in the garden, as music played
and the moon plied the harvest dusk.
You read the poem on a Chinese vase
that stood outside your father's room,
where he dozed in a mandarin dream
of King Gia Long's reposing at Ben Ngu.
We worry that you all are safe.
A house with pillars carved in poems
is floored with green rice fields;
and roofed by all the heavens of this world.

After Our War

After our war, the dismembered bits
—all those pierced eyes, ear slivers, jaw splinters,
gouged lips, odd tibias, skin flaps, and toes—
came squinting, wobbling, jabbering back.

The genitals, of course, were the most bizarre,
inching along roads like glowworms and slugs.
The living wanted them back, but good as new.
The dead, of course, had no use for them.
And the ghosts, the tens of thousands of abandoned
     souls
who had appeared like swamp fog in the city streets,
on the evening altars, and on doorsills of cratered
     homes,
also had no use for the scraps and bits
because, in their opinion, they looked good without
     them.
Since all things naturally return to their source,
these snags and tatters arrived, with immigrant
     uncertainty,
in the United States. It was almost home.
So, now, one can sometimes see a friend or a famous
     man talking
with an extra pair of lips glued and yammering on his
     cheek,
and this is why handshakes are often unpleasant,
why it is better, sometimes, not to look another in the
     eye,
why, at your daughter's breast thickens a hard keloidal
     scar.
After the war, with such Cheshire cats grinning in our
     trees,
will the ancient tales still tell us new truths?
Will the myriad world surrender new metaphor?
After our war, how will love speak?

For Mrs. Cam, Whose Name Means "Printed Silk"

The ancients liked to write of natural beauty.
Ho Chi Minh, "On Reading *The Ten Thousand Poets*"

In Vietnam, poets brushed on printed silk
those poems about clouds, mountains, and love.
But now their poems are cased in steel.

You lived beyond the Pass of Clouds
along the Perfume River, in Hué,
whose name means "lily."

The war has blown away your past.
No poem can call it back.
How does one start over?

You raise your kids in southern California;
run a key punch from 9:00 to 5:00,
and walk the beach each evening,

marveling at curls broken bare in crushed shells,
at the sheen and cracks of laved, salted wood,
at the pearling blues of rock-stuck mussels

all broken, all beautiful, accidents
which remind you of your life, lost friends
and pieces of poems which made you whole.

In tidal pools, the pipers wade
on twiggy legs, stabbing for starfish
with scissoring, poking, needle bills.

The wide Pacific flares in sunset.
Somewhere over there was once your home.
You study the things which start from scratch.

Nicely like a pearl is a poem
begun with an accidental speck
from the ocean of the actual.

A grain, a grit, which once admitted
irritates the mantle of thought
and coats itself in lacquers of the mind.

April 30, 1975

for Bui Ngoc Huong

The evening Nixon called his last troops off,
the church bells tolled across our states.
We leaned on farmhouse porch pilings, our eyes
wandering the lightning bug meadow thick with mist,
and counted tinny peals clanking out
through oaks around the church belltower.
You asked, "Is it peace, or only a bell ringing?"

This night the war has finally ended.
My wife and I sit on a littered park bench
sorting out our shared and separate lives
in the dark, in silence, before a quiet pond
where ducks tug slimy papers and bits of soggy bread.
City lights have reddened the bellies of fumed clouds
like trip flares scorching skies over a city at war.

In whooshing traffic at the park's lit edge,
red brake lights streak to sudden halts:
a ski-masked man staggers through lanes,
maced by a girl he tried to mug.

As he crashes to curb under mercury lamps,
a man snakes towards him, wetting his lips,
twirling the root of his tongue like a dial.

Some kids have burnt a bum on Brooklyn Bridge.
Screaming out of sleep, he flares the causeway.
The war returns like figures in a dream.
In Vietnam, pagodas chime their bells.
"A Clear Mind spreads like the wind.
By the Lo waterfalls, free and high,
you wash away the dust of life."

Dead for Two Years, Erhart Arranges to Meet Me in a Dream

So the cyclo driver,
mantis eyed in mirror glasses,
straddling his blue-and-orange,
pin-striped, lawnmotorized chair—
met me at the corner just as Erhart said.
Neither the driver nor I—slightly fuddled
from having been awakened by the call—
registered much surprise: In dreams,
nearly every night, the dead ring up
and Vietnamese cabbies hustle U.S. streets
in one's post-war, American sleep.
So I just plunked down on the vinyl cushion
and he varoomed a blue cloud all the way to Saigon.

Trouble was, I forgot the address.
The driver stiffened and grew skeptical:
Could this American behave in a dream?
I promised double fare and we zipped
back to the Pittsburgh corner where
—silly forgetful me—I searched

the base of the street lamp on which
I had penciled Erhart's address.
A rain had bled the graphite to a smudge.
Rainwater guttered along the curb.

In Celebration of Spring

Our Asian war is over; others have begun.
Our elders, who tried to mortgage lies,
are disgraced, or dead, and already
the brokers are picking their pockets
for the keys and the credit cards.

In delta swamp in a united Vietnam,
a Marine with a bullfrog for a face,
rots in equatorial heat. An eel
slides through the cage of his bared ribs.
At night, on the old battlefields, ghosts,
like patches of fog, lurk into villages
to maunder on doorsills of cratered homes,
while all across the U.S.A.
the wounded walk about and wonder where to go.

And today, in the simmer of lyric sunlight,
the chrysalis pulses in its mushy cocoon,
under the bark on a gnarled root of an elm.
In the brilliant creek, a minnow flashes
delirious with gnats. The turtle's heart
quickens its taps in the warm bank sludge.
As she chases a frisbee spinning in sunlight,
a girl's breasts bounce full and strong;
a boy's stomach, as he turns, is flat and strong.

Swear by the locust, by dragonflies on ferns,
by the minnow's flash, the tremble of a breast,
by the new earth spongy under our feet:

that as we grow old, we will not grow evil,
that although our garden seeps with sewage,
and our elders think it's up for auction—swear
by this dazzle that does not wish to leave us—
that we will be keepers of a garden, nonetheless.

News Update

*for Erhart, Gitelson, Flynn and Stone,
happily dead and gone.*

Well, here I am in the *Centre Daily Times*
back to back with the page one refugees
fleeing the crossfire, pirates, starvation.
Familiar faces. We followed them
through defoliated forests, cratered fields,
past the blasted water buffalo,
the shredded tree lines, the human head
dropped on the dusty road, eyes open,
the dusty road which called you all to death.

One skims the memory like a moviola
editing out the candid shots: Sean Flynn
dropping his camera and grabbing a gun
to muster the charge and retake the hill.
"That boy," the black corporal said,
"do in real life what his daddy do in movies."
Dana Stone, in an odd moment of mercy,
sneaking off from Green Beret assassins
to the boy they left for dead in the jungle.
Afraid of the pistol's report, Stone shut his eyes
and collapsed the kid's throat with a bayonet.
Or, Erhart, sitting on his motorcycle
smiling and stoned in the Free Strike Zone
as he filmed the ammo explosion at Lai Khe.

It wasn't just a macho game. Marie-Laure de Decker
photographed the man aflame on the public lawn.
She wept and shook and cranked her Pentax
until a cop smashed it to the street. Then
there was the girl returned from captivity
with a steel comb fashioned from a melted-down tank,
or some such cliché, and engraved: "To Sandra
From the People's Fifth Battalion, Best Wishes."

Christ, most of them are long dead. Tim Page
wobbles around with a steel plate in his head.
Gitelson roamed the Delta in cut-away blue jeans
like a hippy Johnny Appleseed with a burlap sack
full of seeds and mimeographed tips for farmers
until we pulled him from the canal. His brains
leaked on my hands and knee. Or me, yours truly,
agape in the Burn Ward in Da Nang, a quonset hut,
a half a garbage can that smelled like Burger King,
listening to whimpers and nitrate fizzing on flesh
in a silence that simmered like a fly in a wound.

And here I am, ten years later,
written up in the local small town press
for popping a loud-mouth punk in the choppers.
Oh, big sighs. Windy sighs. And ghostly laughter.

Thoughts Before Dawn

for Mary Bui Thi Khuy, 1944–1969

The bare oaks rock and snowcrust tumbles down
while squirrels snug down in windy nests
swaying under stars above the frozen earth.

The creaking eave woke me, thinking of you
crushed by a truck thirteen years ago
when the drunk ARVN lost the wheel.

We brought to better care the nearly lost,
the boy burned by white phosphorus, chin
glued to his chest; the scalped girl;
the triple amputee from the road-mined bus;
the kid without a jaw; the one with no nose.
You never wept in front of them, but waited
until the gurney rolled them into surgery.
I guess that's what amazed me most.
Why didn't you fall apart or quit?

Once, we flew two patched kids home,
getting in by Army chopper,
a Huey Black Cat that skimmed the sea.
When the gunner opened up on a whale
you closed your eyes and covered your ears
and your small body shook in your silk ao dai.
Oh, Mary. In this arctic night, awake in my bed
I rehearse your smile, bright white teeth,
the funny way you rode your Honda 50, perched
so straight, silky hair bunned up in a brim hat,
front brim blown back, and dark glasses.
Brave woman, I hope you never saw the truck.

Story

The guy picked me up north of Santa Fe
where the red hills, dotted with piñon,
loop down from the Divide into mesas and plain.
I was standing out there—just me, my pack,
and the gila monsters—when he hauled his Buick

off the road in a sputter of cinders and dust.
And got out, a gray-bearded, 6-foot, 300-pounder,
who stretched and said, "Do you want to drive?"
So I drove and he told me the story of his life.
How his father was a Russian Jew who got zapped
by the Mob during Prohibition, how he quit school
at fifteen and got a job as a DJ in Detroit,
how he sold flatware on the road and made a mint,
how he respected his wife, but didn't love her,
how he hit it big in radio and tv, how he fell in love,
how he found himself, at 50, in intensive care
where his wife, his kids, his girlfriend, and his rabbi
huddled in silence about his bed when his doctor
came in and whispered that maybe he ought to ask
the wife and the girlfriend to alternate visits
'because it wasn't too good for his heart.'
"What about your kids?" I asked. "What do they
    do?"
"My daughter runs our store. My son is dead."
He studied a distant peak and didn't continue.
"What did he die of?"—"He died of suicide.
. . . No, that's not right. Nixon killed him.
My son was a sweet kid, hated guns and violence
and then, during that fucking war, he hijacked a plane
and flew it to Cuba. He shot himself in Havana."
He studied the peak, then grinned and said,
"Brave little fucker, wasn't he?" I nodded.

That night, camping in a patch of mesquite and pine,
as I rocked a log to roll it towards my fire,
I saw a mouse squashed in its nest of willow down.
Its brave heart thumped as I held it in my hand
where it skittered to escape just before it died.
I laid it down by the glow of the campfire
which flickered like a lamp in the circling trees.
In the distance, the highway whined like gnats,
and, in the east, a full moon was on the rise.

JAN BARRY

In the Footsteps of Genghis Khan

There, where a French legionnaire
once walked patrol
around the flightline perimeter of the airfield
at Nha Trang,
ten years later I walked,
an American expeditionary forces
soldier on night guard duty
at Nha Trang,
occupied even earlier,
twenty years before
(a year more than my nineteen),
by the Japanese.

Unhaunted by the ghosts, living and dead
among us
in the red tile-roofed French barracks
or listening in on the old Japanese telephone line
to Saigon,
we went about our military duties,
setting up special forces headquarters
where once a French Foreign Legion post had been,
oblivious to the irony
of Americans walking in the footsteps
of Genghis Khan.

Unencumbered by history,
our own or that of 13th-century Mongol armies
long since fled or buried

by the Vietnamese,
in Nha Trang, in 1962, we just did our jobs:
replacing kepis with berets, "Ah so!" with "Gawd!
Damn!"

Nights in Nha Trang

The girls,
the girls of
Nha Trang
ply their trade
every night
along the beach

"Monique,
Monique come
ti ti
Monique
come you
ti ti"

The peanut
girls,
twelve
and thirteen
singing

"You buy
mango,
you buy me?
You buy
mango,
you buy
me?"

All
selling the
fruit
of Nha
Trang
every night
along the
dark

crescent
beach

"You buy
Saigon tea,
you buy
me?
You buy me
one
Saigon tea?"

A Nun in Ninh Hoa

It was quite a sight for a boy from Tennessee:
a Buddhist nun dressed in fire
sitting proudly amid a solemn, silent crowd,
flames and a smoke plume her terrible costume.

Riding shotgun on a fuel truck convoy,
"just along for the ride,"
Jimmy Sharpe saw a sight this morning
beyond any experience he can describe.

She sat smiling as though mocking the flames.
Her hands, held together in prayer,
slowly parted. Suddenly, she drooped,
sat up, then wilted in the fire.

Safe back at the base, Jimmy's chatter
circled the nightmare he still could taste.
He grinned—shivered—then softly swore:
"Jeesus! How'd we get in this crazy place?"

Floating Petals

See: here, the bougainvillea;
there, the cactus and palm—
    here: the lotus flower:
    there, the bomb-shattered bamboo

of viet-nam

severed flowers, sharded fronds:
    floating in shrapnel,
    sealed in napalm.

Green Hell, Green Death

Green hell of the jungle:
    green fire, green death,
    green ghosts,
    green,
grim bodies

Green jungle all around: hot,
    full of death,
    fox-fire,
    floating ghosts,
ghosts of the quick and the dead

Green hell: green bodies:
    the living, from pallor and dirt
    the dying, from gasping breath
    the dead, from blood-drained
wounds: all in green uniforms

Other green bodies: hidden in
the green jungle
in green camouflage
and green branches and twigs:
green leaves covering quick, green limbs

Green hell: green jungle: green bodies:
green leaves stalking
green uniforms hunting
green limbs
in the growth of the ghost jungle

Green ghosts: flitting through green
trees—
green fire: from green fingers
on green guns—
green jungle: green hellfire: green death

Harvest Moon

Pumpkins' crooked grins
on Halloween window ledges
hide candle flames of bamboo villages . . .

glowing behind the orange
decapitated skulls of Asians
staring at shouting masked children
dressed as little spirits of pirates . . .

waving drooping bags of loot
in wild night chases
with soldiers pilgrims witches
skeletons cowboys and revived "Indians."

* * *

Here where our farms and towns,
factories and cities and highways lie,
the civilizations that we buried
rise with the harvest moon.

On a city sidewalk gangs of stick-armed
tricksters steal candy from younger ones,
across a quiet village street
a spinster's favorite privy spills,

while down the road
small shapes scatter from a farm
as a field of hay goes up in flames.

Lessons

"What's a patriot, Dad?
Hey, Dad! 'Earth to Dad—
Earth to Dad!'
Get your nose out of
your newspaper!
Help me with my homework!
What's a patriot, Dad?"

"Well, I guess, a person
who loves the land.
Although some people act as if
a patriot's a man
who hates another land."

"Hey, Dad! Don't
give me a lecture—
all I need's
a word! Just a word!
What's a veteran, Dad?
Hey, Dad! DAD!"

* * *

"A veteran's what your
father is—" his mother
chimed in, clear across the room.

"Oh, I got it:
somebody who's always out
of work, home with us
kids—huh, Dad?
Is that what a veteran is?"

"Yep—" Dad got out,
remembering suddenly
the time his youngest son
had stopped breathing
right here at the kitchen table
(with this oldest son screaming,
"Nicky's dead! Nicky's dead!")
and the frantic fight
to find a sign of life,
while dialing the emergency number
for an ambulance.

"What's war? Dad!
You know, Dad! War—war!
Dad! What the hell's war?"

And old Dad blurted out,
still thinking of the desperate
battle one desperate night
to save the baby's life:
"Ten minutes of terror,
after twenty years of anticipation,
and then twenty years of worrying
'when's it going to happen
again?' "

R. L. BARTH

The Insert

Our view of sky, jungle, and fields constricts
Into a sink hole covered with saw-grass

Undulating, soon whipped slant as the chopper
Hovers at four feet. Rapt, boot deep in slime,

We deploy ourselves in loose perimeter,
Listening for incoming rockets above

The thump of rotor blades; edgy for contact,
Junkies of terror impatient to shoot up.

Nothing moves, nothing sounds; then, single file,
We move across a stream-bed toward high ground.

The terror of the insert's quickly over.
Too quickly . . . And more quickly every time . . .

Letter from An Hoc (4), by a Seedbed

Judge of the nations, spare us yet,
Lest we forget—lest we forget!
RUDYARD KIPLING

1

Some distance away
you can see, across paddies and woods,

32

in this stunned glare of mid-day,
    six green shades like moods

      that betray the villes
we have been patrolling since first light,
    humping for the far foothills—
        as if in mad flight

      from the privation
of palm-leaf huts, wood hoes, small pieces
    of china, and eyes that shun
        our faceless faces.

2

      There are no young men:
they are hiding, Viet Cong, or dead.
    Only the old folk, children
      and empty-breasted
      mothers still remain,
survivors among all the wreckage.
    Are they trying to retain
      some hold? or to edge

      from a commitment,
patiently waiting out their desire?
    I don't know. Once arrogant,
      bringing aid, the fire

      of napalm, and lead,
I become one of their witnesses
    to history: this seedbed,
      with its crevices

      sluicing through earth's crust;
this seedbed, like a dry pod shaken
    over a dead land, like lust
      without a woman.

P.O.W.s

Lieutenant Gilbert took us down the hill
This morning at first light, sweeping a ville
For sympathizers. I am guarding two
Of them, a mama-san and her child, who
Squat, fingers quick, blindfolded, loosely bound.
It's odd, but neither makes the smallest sound,
Kneading this silence that I cannot fill.

Postscript

At last, the senses sharpen. All around,
I listen closely. Under the dull sound
Of distant artillery, and the shrieking planes
Diving with napalm; under the dry crack
Of automatic rifles; at the back
Of consciousness, almost, a sound remains:
Mud sucking at bare feet as they are going
Between the rice shoots. Nearly silent. Knowing.

STEPHEN BERG

May 1970

Thirteen faces waiting to be born
and nothing to say on this Monday morning,
the schools closed, rain, the new killing.
What do the crickets hear when I lie down on them
in the grass? My hands sinking?
I'd go to Jesus Christ like Arina, the woman
from the Hotel Madrid in Babel's story who was
    knocked-up
and beaten across the belly with a belt
by Seryoga, the janitor, I'd talk to God
like she did and hear Him say "You cannot kiss
your own ear . . ." and be turned into an angel
with wings made from the sighs of babies,
I'd fuck the father of my child until he smothered
and Christ cursed me for killing one of His angels,
I'd make Christ weep for me, like she did,
if I could bring us back,
because who else does this kind of thing?
who else needs to be forgiven?
This morning we decided to list our bad dreams
in a letter to Nixon, beginning "Dear Mother,
we don't like these dreams, we can't stand them,
we know you caused them, we want you to take them
    back . . .
signed thirteen students without wings
who have arms that don't lift,
feet that lie flat on the ground and freeze,
hands that tremble and go nowhere,

lips as tender as the passages of birth,
anger in the snapping of wings.''
I'd put my mouth against theirs but they don't breathe,
and it goes on like this,
I'd lift up each skirt and let my head slide back in,
like disciples who worship revelation in The Mother,
asking ''Is this the wound, is this . . . ?''

D. C. BERRY

The sun   goes
       down
   a different way when

                you
are lungshot in a rice
paddy and you
are taking a drink of
your own unhomeostatic
globules each

Time

you swallow a pail
of air   pumping like you
were

bailing out the whole
world   throw
  ing it in your leak
   ing   collapsible lung
that won't hold even
a good quart   and on
top of that   the sun
goes down

      Bang

ing the lung completely
flat.

• • •

They say Spring came
        in May when it came   may
be.   but a boy was dead then
        shot in the gut and gray
liver by   the victor
        Charley.

the boy's pa couldn't under
stand   spring killin
      of his boy—

"My God may
be he ain't really dead."
buried in the May
mound in the Cemetery.

the boy's ma said may
be   he's one of the Lord's
pretty flowers'll rise
resurrection day—
      "God woman ain't
no dead bulb gonna rise this May
never! God
      pity you Martha!"

• • •

The perfume on the Oriental
      morning

blows from the broken flowers
taken
         from their roots by the

mourning   mamasan—

              lies
upon my nose's   tongue

like a sweet monsoon
with no flood to perform
nor despair to flood.

     the mamasan
walking about the dawn
as if   the message lately received
     has broken her body
     from its root—
walks
stiff
as on her
knees instead of her feet.

     she drops an herb
     in the ancient vase
to heal the death
     of the flowers   hers

must grow more before

it dies.

• • •

If I'm zapped   bury me
with a
comicbook   let

Tennyson keep his
buried William Shakespeare   put

a comic
on my   chest   and   shovel
me   overtight

        in my new life I'll be

Clark Kent

instead
of

Superman.

• • •

Sgt. Sam Sublime never died
when he was killed cause he kept
his heart in a blue
guitar. Snapped.

And I know cause I know
exactly where he was when
he put himself like a big black

beautiful bomb into that blue guitar
and got down on God!
Amighty! Got
down on a loin funky nigger
song that drove the snakes
in Oriental music   crazy.

And we would sit there holding on
to the Orient till our pulses
fell in with slow zooms in the
silent pounding of his song
and then we were gone where our ankles
weren't afraid of stepping on neither
the razor/horizon nor a booby
trap trip wire—
                    dancing like
an OD Caterpillar
in Sam's blood ballad
where we were safe from the
gooks and snakes.

Till a string broke
and they mailed Sam
home. Said
his spinal chord was
knocked completely out of tune
by the whack of a 10,000
pound bomb
from a B-52.

ROBERT BLY

Counting Small-Boned Bodies

Let's count the bodies over again.

If we could only make the bodies smaller,
The size of skulls,
We could make a whole plain white with skulls in the
    moonlight!

If we could only make the bodies smaller,
Maybe we could get
A whole year's kill in front of us on a desk!

If we could only make the bodies smaller,
We could fit
A body into a finger-ring, for a keepsake forever.

At a March against the Vietnam War

Washington, November 27, 1965

Newspapers rise high in the air over Maryland

We walk about, bundled in coats
        and sweaters in the late November sun

Looking down, I see feet moving

Calmly, gaily,
Almost as if separated from their bodies

But there is something moving in the dark somewhere
Just beyond
The edge of our eyes: a boat
Covered with machine guns
Moving along under the trees

It is black,
The hand reaches out
And cannot touch it—
It is that darkness among pine boughs
That the Puritans brushed
As they went out to kill turkeys

At the edge of the jungle clearing
It explodes
On the ground

We long to abase ourselves

We have carried around this cup of darkness
We have longed to pour it over our heads

We make war
Like a man anointing himself

Section VI of "The Teeth Mother Naked at Last"

But if one of those children came near that we have set
    on fire,
came toward you like a gray barn, walking,
you would howl like a wind tunnel in a hurricane,

43

you would tear at your shirt with blue hands,
you would drive over your own child's wagon trying to
    back up,
the pupils of your eyes would go wild—

If a child came by burning, you would dance on a
    lawn,
trying to leap into the air, digging into your cheeks,
you would ram your head against the wall of your
    bedroom
like a bull penned too long in his moody pen—

If one of those children came toward me with both
    hands
in the air, fire rising along both elbows,
I would suddenly go back to my animal brain,
I would drop on all fours, screaming,
my vocal chords would turn blue, so would yours,
it would be two days before I could play with my own
    children again.

IGOR BOBROWSKY

The Journey

Where were you bound for, unknown man,
wobbling along on bony legs beneath your load,
could you not feel the blind eyes stare upon your back
or smell the madness in the air around you?

Why did you try so hard to get where you were going,
racing the creeping night to your poor bowl of rice?
Did you not hear the silent laughing scream behind you
that would not wait, or listen to replies?

The load's not heavy any more for you now, is it?
And the journey's not as urgent now as then it
    seemed— .
for night's caught up and long since overtaken you
and your poor bowl of rice
                    has long ago grown cold . . .

Free Fire Zone

Trembling and sobbing
you crawl out of your hole
brown grime encrusted on your face,
brittle white hair touched gently by the wind.

And begging you fall down on your knees
and raise your wizened hands in supplication

to what stands mute in us, and cold to all your needs—
which kicks and prods you back upon your feet.

You stumble, dazed, between the holes
                    into the empty field beyond
and fall, and turn, and fall and cry again at us . . .
And then as flame comes blazing to engulf you from
    the sky
I wonder why
                    you ever bothered
                                        ever being born.

D. F. BROWN

Coming Home

for Janice Bolton

There is something I want to say
Not anything you need believe
But there is no thunder here
And the silence
Nothing forgives

I march out vagrant
A culprit at home nowhere
Or everywhere
Dancing stealth
Into living rooms

Someone has stacked his books
Records, souvenirs, pretending
This will always be light
And zoned residential

Patrols

This is where stacking pays off.
Invent numbers each time you need one.
Sunlight more than names, any name.
Someplace, he put them—
The days you watch good friends die

The world keeps moving
Hard notes cut light
Limbs branching, the vines
They hold it all together—
Someone says the war is over
"Look how it ended"—the end

What we say for the nights
I could run naked taking hills
From the small dark people

You always hear
How they drag their dead away
And who kept score

Returning Fire

for Bruce Weigl and Ngo Vinh Long

Hell hath no power over pagans.
This is still life.
                              RIMBAUD

what we think
                we remember
empty
        waiting in the rain
for the last plane
                        you know
you were there
                watching
each drop collect dust
                        as if getting wet
made a difference
                say the names

take any way back
                down a hot tropic
trail to good soldiers
                        slopped in mud
in the ache
            among believers
paint your face green
                    and pretend
it's too much
            like summer picnics
something
            the kids want to show you
it happens
            like no one can plan
maybe
        only chance to know bravery
you think so
            they drown in it
you can't tell
            people from weeds
some are wide receivers
                        others hug the ground
the sergeant walks around
                        like he's running
for election
            talks of growing
old surviving
            each day
a cold six pack
            the evening news
football season
            ends on Sunday
a woman sings the anthem
                    for nothing
the rest cheering
                you bought tickets
you want to
        believe in Cézanne

life underlined
                scored yellow
you remember that part
                you keep going
once to the river
                in spring
every weekend
                through summer
true visitor
                they don't know
the season
                why they sacrificed
the trees for you
                children of real travelers
they brush mornings
                and evening the scar
cut in the west
                small circle from here
sandbagged
                they whisper themselves
dusk in the jungle
                for tongues so pure
and gone to god
                you call them
with a motion
                a little hike
a little while longer
                you want them
to slip from green
                clothes wet boots
with plenty hot water
                you would steam off mud
get them ready for bed
                it isn't night
empty spaces
                or the tropics
green is nothing
                it holds the trees

and stops sky
                    it isn't guns
or the ammo
                    they sleep on knowing
the other side
                    creased
and still white
                    they never come back
soaked off into jungle
                              they rise only
in the rough
                    second growth
that follows

When I Am 19 I Was a Medic

for Lee, who sculpts light

All day I always want to know
the angle, the safest approach.
I want to know the right time
to go in. Who is in front
of me, who is behind.
When the last shots were fired,
what azimuth will get me out,
the nearest landing zone.

Each night I lay out all my stuff:
morphine, bandages at my shoulder,
just below, parallel, my rifle.
I sleep strapped to a .45,
bleached into my fear.
I do this under the biggest tree,
some nights I dig
in saying my wife's name
over and over.

* * *

I can tell true stories
from the jungle. I never mention
the fun, our sense of humor
embarrasses me. Something
warped it out of place
and bent I drag it along—
keeping track of time spent,
measure what I think we have left.

Now they tell me something else—
I've heard it all before
sliding through the grass
to get here.

Illumination

no sunrise here   three layers of green
give a day a lime glow   evening lasts five
grey minutes   the dark lasts all night
lighting a smoke marks the spot for anybody
everything is a dead giveaway

  the new L T dreams up some movement
he has to see   he is truly possessed
has been crying for his girl   she is all
he needs but a little light in the jungle
will make it   go away   he radios base
crank up the 105s   fire illumination

  a we-know-they-know-where-we-are-at
I hope we don't find them   I've been there
seen the pictures

I Was Dancing Alone in Binh Dinh Province

for John Jacobson

There is an award for this,
a decoration, something
they want us to believe.

All flanks covered, always
the point man steps out,
counts each move glancing
for movement he can shoot.
Next two men pull slack—
spaced five meters any blast
will get only one.

Someone will handle the radio.
Someone will carry Band-Aids.
Someone will have a map, compass

the number—his plumb line ignores the hill,
brown paddies, blue river, shallow
deep—it takes too many
helicopters
to get here
I don't trust air
to find the place
less a matter of time
sinks into cramps
an ache   in my gut
I lose track with these guys
how gentle they are
rattles with machine guns

                        * * *

Whoever holds title to this
has a handful
soil hearts move through

Eating the Forest

If I am alive in the morning
then I am alive in the dream
                        RIMBAUD

Background is instrumental
mountains start there
a seven year old could draw this—
highlands angle above paddies
block the valley water
is a curl, brown river, everything
green in two shades—
the darkest fills in
edges, covering heroes, marks
out each stalk rising, the other
catches light in corners
turning heat—we live
with the killing, fight
every war we were
raised to fight
an enemy we couldn't see
music going like crazy
on both sides
we rummaged our hearts
forget words
hum the tune

It all depends on forty men
automatic rifles

grenades
faces painted green—
the man behind me is twenty feet away
circles join us, sandbagged
mines point from the spot
we guard with our lives
I keep count for them
the cases—malaria,
hepatitis, VD, purple
hearts, red marks,
red marks we live
soak off into jungle
every day each man
the small, white antimalarial pill
fifty-two Mondays the big orange tablet
I have to go on
nothing got to die

We were killing ourselves
uphill
a trail to the ridge
through jungle
uphill
there was no noise
even the birds keep quiet
uphill
the trail through
no noise, we were
jungle, birds
the ridge
uphill
no one would fall
jungle
hills with their numbers
valleys with names

We think we are
ready awake

all night the dead
snap back on legs
they had the day before
bleached into dreams
we talk sweet for them
working their slow way around
new at being dead, young
and nervous kick
the dirt, try wiping
off mud, and still
they carry everything—
ammo, the charges, flares
cut sharp floating
angles, they don't kill
shadows, we are cut-outs,
the dead stay for contrast
each one on point
calling out code
for his presence
they don't need music
days have no names
the 10,000 versions
of the war are one
in the great, late All-Night
they keep track in our sleep
—visibility
far off standing
light thick sound
tracked each flash
crosses soldiers,
trained to sleep
where the moon sinks
and bring the darkness home

D. F. Brown

Still Later There Are War Stories

For those who think of us, not as we were
RANDALL JARRELL

1

Another buddy dead.
There is enough dying—
Gary Cooper will
ride up, slow and easy
slide off his horse
without firing a shot
save us all.

It is a matter of waiting.
We grow old counting the year
in days, one by one
each morning ritual marks
one more, one less—
the plane has yet to land.

2

Down freeways, past federal cemetery flags
half masted, dark green lawn,
the watered rows of stone—I could have
come home—November five—to a decade
recounting days since, another
waiting above jungle trails
for then we hope never to see—
field hospital beds, orthopedic surgeons
saving lives, fifteen minutes away . . . . . .

* * *

Daily boy scout excursions
through brush so thick
one hour hacking brings you
twenty feet closer to home,
down a new tropic trail. The jungle
loaded, nobody
comes away in one piece.

First Person—1981

there are days I have to pretend
I am someone else to get out of bed
make all the necessary noises
remember how it ended, how the end
is still caught in so many

I get through these days
The lowest part of the jungle
a pale green gnarl
roots and vines
searching for sunlight
through
this tangle

STEVEN FORD BROWN

After the Vietnam War

sometimes
on windless nights
when the moon glows
like a tv set in a dark room
the vietnam dead rise

bodyless heads arms & legs
skitter down pock marked roads
like great hordes
of mutilated rats
in the villages
small dark women kneel
on the dirt floors
of huts

they cut their black hair
rub ashes on foreheads
their cries are almost human

THOMAS BRUSH

Waiting for the End of the War

Trying to sleep by the lake
Is like looking for something
You haven't seen in years. Your hands
Disappear in the dark. You know
Where they should be, floating quietly in the still air,
Talking softly at the juncture of your wrists,
But you are unable to see or touch them. The years are
    falling away
Behind you, like your hands, like the trail
Of down from the sleeping bag, the thin
White circles on the wet grass. And you know there is
    nothing
You can do but go on
Looking and the ground, at the edge of sleep, whispers
Here, under here . . .

Again

Though the war has been over for years and nothing is
    dropping out
Of the stone side of the sky to send you back across the
    nearest border
Except the broken promise of snow, slowly filling the
    square yard
In front of you, and the old lies as familiar as books or
    the weather,

You still won't understand. You see the doors broken
    open again,
The water blacken and go bad, and children crouched
    like old men
Under trees and bridges. You imagine women in the
    last sad act
Of war, wandering through the ruins of their lives,
    carrying blankets
And sacks of food, the men gone, and the torn sheets
    of flame
Over everything.

CHRISTOPHER BURSK

Lies

My son and I kiss the same woman goodbye.
We are meeting thousands in the dark of the Capital.
This is the first lie:
that I wish to bring peace to anyone
besides those with me now in the lamp's small territory.

Soon we'll be marching down a wide street ending in
    flags
and marble—and dawn, huge and official
turning the white stone glistening.
We shade our eyes, march into the dazzle
as if light were another kind of government.

This is the second lie:
that the men inside the building hate the light,
have been hurt so deeply they'd have the world hurt.
With them are my father, my brother,
gentle, considerate men,

and though I love them, I rise with others against them.
This is the third lie:
that we have weapons they don't: a love for children,
a concern for the planet.
My boy and I welcome the sun on the backs of our
    necks,

we need it there
as we walk into the darkness between buildings.

The police wait for us.
Soon they'll raise their arms and bring down
the shadows we expect.

This is the fourth lie:
that these men like to wield the darkness.
The fifth lie: that they have not chosen to.
Mother and wife, the person we love most in the
   world,
has sent instructions:

keep away from the violence.
This is the sixth lie: that we can.
The seventh: that we wish to.
We move closer to the damage, lurk in its shade
as if hearing the screams

seeing the blood, we might understand.
The eighth lie is that we do.
We'd thought by walking in great sunlit masses
before those who began this war
we might end it. We lift the sun in our hands

as if to show the men in small groups gathering at the
   windows
there is another government.
The ninth lie is that they do not know this,
are not grateful like us for free passage on the earth,
the sun's generosity.

The tenth lie is the hardest.
That we are in no danger, from these men,
that you are in no danger, my son,
from the faithful, the earnest, from friend, brother,
or father.

MARYLIN BUTLER

Listen

She said she would marry him
if he would catch hold of the
sunflowers growing in the field,
if he would yield to the pain
of their being uprooted in his hands,
if he would lift them with his words,
with strands of beads becoming words.

"Forgive me the bright green fronds,"
he answered, "the bare skin and veins
of my hands. I will pick the flowers
with the yellow eyes, the lifted lips.
My face is rough with scars
if I press you against it.
I suppose you can tell me
what I do not see myself."

"Who is the equal of anyone?"

"Come, we will run together.
Whatever we catch, that is the reason
why we are here."

"How do you wish to live,
now that you've returned?"

And they both paused,
listening.

JOSEPH CADY

Starting 1973:
What to Do Now that Peace Has Been Announced

At the end of January you will see again
the man you had been wanting to meet for months
and at last you'll go up and say you'd like to meet him.

This man will go home with you later from the bar
after saying that he hardly ever goes home with
    anyone anymore.
You will tell him he is beautiful;
he will tell you you are beautiful;
you will sleep side by side every night for two months.

Then at Easter this lover
will knock you breathless and leave you:
he will say that he never felt joy in the relationship;
he will tell you he can no longer hold in his violence.

HAYDEN CARRUTH

On Being Asked to Write a Poem
Against the War in Vietnam

Well I have and in fact
more than one and I'll
tell you this too

I wrote one against
Algeria that nightmare
and another against

Korea and another
against the one
I was in

and I don't remember
how many against
the three

when I was a boy
Abyssinia Spain and
Harlan County

and not one
breath was restored
to one

shattered throat
mans womans or childs
not one not

one
but death went on and on
never looking aside

except now and then like a child
with a furtive half-smile
to make sure I was noticing.

RON CARTER

Vietnam Dream

Sometimes still   in my deepest sleep
Someone orders "Turn"   and we turn.
The ship swings lazily   like a great log
Caught in a current,   and
The guns point to something I cannot see.

Then someone orders "Fire"   and we fire,
The first shell spinning out of the barrel
Like a football   thrown for a gain.
Where it touches the earth
Smoke puffs   like popcorn.

And then   all is still.
I have been ready now for years,
Waiting the order that never came,
The sneer of cold command,
The Jews lined up at the bathhouse door.

I cannot see beyond that moment
Whether   shaking my head   I turn
Away   or whether   when someone
orders
"Kill"   I kill.

RAY CATINA

Negotiations

We give them chocolate bars
and they say Thank You GI san sir
and they sell you their sister

Two weeks later you can't walk
can't piss
can't think straight
and your balls are on fire

The Medic Man says you've got the Black Death
there's no known cure

and just when you think he's maybe
like shitting you
they take out all these needles and knives
like they're going to cut

and you're saying hey wait a minute
hold on
let's talk

but it's too late for that

Philosophy

There was no
getting around it
Air Head said
You stepped into the
noose everytime you
took a breath
in this place
You might as well do
Lucky Strikes, Jack Daniels
and dope everytime you can
You ain't getting
to heaven on any pass
the Army ever signed but
they had a weird habit
of messing up your
short time forever
Better to be wild drunk
and crazy around here
so whenever whatever it was
happened at least you'd
be able to blend right in

HORACE COLEMAN

OK Corral East
Brothers in the Nam

Sgt. Christopher and I are
in Khanh Hoi down by the docks
in the Blues Bar where the women
are brown and there is no Saigon Tea
making our nightly HIT—'Hore Inspection Tour
watching the black   digging night sights
   soul sounds   getting tight

the grunts in the corner raise undisturbed hell
the timid white MP has his freckles pale
as he walks past the high dude
in the doorway in his lavender jump-suit
to remind the mama-san quietly of curfew
    he chokes on the weed smoke
    he sees nothing his color here
and he fingers his army rosary   his .45

but this is not Cleveland or Chicago
he can't cringe any one here and our
gazes like brown punji stakes impale him

we have all killed something recently
we know who owns the night
and carry darkness with us

Night Flare Drop, Tan Son Nhut

It is Tet
    some Vietnamese excuse for fireworks
and the war sneaks into Saigon
while young girls from villages in the Delta
    who have learned to use make-up and read comic
  books
suck off fat Air Force colonels
    All is joy
Roman candles chase tracers
Little rockets bark at dancing dragons
In the foreign cemetery
    at the entrance to the base
dying soldiers are having a colorful fire fight
Six Vietnamese MPs
                    eager to watch
run into a mine field
    and throw yellow confetti for yards
in 100 P Alley the boy pimps laugh
    and sell three-day-old sandwiches
    to Americans afraid to come out of their rooms
For the first time in years no chauffeur-driven
    Mercedes bull through the streets
And trapped in the bar at the Officers' Open Mess
off-duty pilots
                    in dirty flight suits
stand in front of the air-conditioners
    sweating
Overhead frightened planes circle
    shedding magnesium tears that
    burn deep holes in the night
But the dark
                    like the VC   always comes back

Remembrance of Things Past

mortars are
the devil coughing
napalm?
Baudelaire never had
such flowers
such bright fleur de lis
such evil

claymores
shatter more than bones

when they attacked we
killed them dreams and all
we thought

we fired artillery   they
shot hatred back

when we burned their bones
they loathed us still   dying
still trying to get their crisp
black fingers on our white throats

In Ca Mau

in Ca Mau
the women sweep the canal with their oars
on the way to the floating fruit market
bananas
pineapples

grapes with husks stacked in slender sampans
the Americans in Ca Mau eat tin-skinned food
play prostitute roulette clap
                                        syph
                                        rigid love
with rifles under the bed in Ca Mau

the people race bicycles on Sundays
children play soccer on the parade square
the Americans don't come
pigs walk the streets alone
GIs ride six to a fast jeep

they pacify the forest of U Minh
with five-hundred-pound bombs
that fall five miles and shake
the yellow palm-thatched huts and
the yellowed stucco houses and the
yellow tent O Club of Ca Mau

they hunt communist water buffalo
with quad .50s and infra-red
they scream howitzers at suspicious rice
but one bullet
makes a helicopter a shotgunned duck
one rocket trips the man-blind radar
off its legs and the Americans
leave and the women sweep
after them in Ca Mau

A Black Soldier Remembers

My Saigon daughter I saw only once
standing in the dusty square
across from the Brink's BOQ/PX

in back of the National Assembly
next to the ugly statue of
the crouching marines facing
the fish pond the VC blew up
during Tet.

The amputee beggars watch us.
The same color and the same eyes.
She does not offer me one of the
silly hats she sells Americans and
I have nothing she needs but
the sad smile she already has.

A Downed Black Pilot Learns
How to Fly

"now that the war is over
we'll have to kill each other again
but I'll send my medals to Hanoi
and let them make bullets if
they'll ship my leg back and
if they mail me an ash tray
made from my F4C they can keep
the napalm as a bonus. Next time
I'll wait and see if they've declared
war on me—or just America."

FRANK A. CROSS, JR.

Gliding Baskets

"Eight Six Foxtrot—Eight Six Foxtrot.
This is One One Zulu. Over."

    The woman in blue
    Carried the weight swiftly, with grace,
    Her face hidden by her
    Conical rice straw hat.

"One One Zulu—this is Eight Six Foxtrot. Go."
"Roger Eight Six. I have Fire Mission.
Dink in the open, Grid: Bravo Sierra,
Five Six Niner, Four Six Five, Range:
Three thousand, Proximity: Eight hundred. Over"

    The two heavy baskets
    Balanced on tips
    Of the springing Chogi stick
    Glided close to the hard smooth path.

"Read back, One One Zulu."
"Roger Copy, Eight Six."
"Shot, on the way, wait."
"Shot out, Eight Six."

    A sighing 105 mm round slides through its
      parabola
    Then the explosive tearing at the steel which
      surrounds it,
    And the shrapnel catches the gliding baskets,

Frank A. Cross, Jr.

And they crumple with the woman in blue.

near An Trang
August 14, 1969

The Fifty Gunner

It came to his palms,
And to his thumbs
Pressed hard
Against the trigger.

It came through
His hands,
And up his arms,
And across his shoulders.

Then, the telegraphed recoils
Set bouncing
The peace medallion
Dangling on his chest.

From his muzzle,
The huge bullets
Ripped flesh
From the running targets.

Rice Will Grow Again

We were walking
On the dikes
Like damn fools—
Steppin over dud rounds.

* * *

Mitch was steppin light
When he saw the farmer.
    The farmer:
    With black shirt
    And shorts.
    Up to his knees
    In the muck
    Rice shoots in one hand,
    The other darting
    Under the water
    And into the muck
    To plant new life.

Mitch saw the farmer's hand
Going down again
With another
        Shoot
            But the hand
            Never came up
            Again—
After Mitch
Ripped the farmer up the middle
With a burst of sixteen.
We passed the farmer,
As we walked
Along the dike, and
I saw rice shoots
Still clutched in one hand.
He bubbled strange words
Through the blood
In his mouth.
Bong, the scout,
Told us the farmer
Said:
    "Damn you
    The rice will
    Grow again!"

* * *

Sometimes,
On dark nights
In Kansas,
The farmer comes to
            Mitch's bed:
And plants rice shoots
            all around.

When Chicken Man Came Home to Roost

You had a good home when you left!
        —yer right!
You had a good car when you left!
        —yer right!
You had a good girl when you left!
        —yer right!
JODY was there when you left!
        —yer right!
Drill Mill's favorite marching jive.

1
(He still wore the OD tee shirt
With the sleeves ripped off.)
Chicken Man flapped
Down the end of the bar
—a Sat-tray night—
And taps a beer from Jody
(Who was there when he left.)
       Jody asks:
"Where ya been man?
Ain't seen ya near a year!"
       Chicken Man squawks:
"Ya got a roger copy Smack!"
       Jody:

"Don't get ripped man—
I just wondered where ya been."
          Chicken Man:
"Down on that jungle floor!"
And he ran out the bar,
—Jungle rot festering,
  Long hair flying
Screaming:
  "Sam said getcher guns!"

Jody just slowly shook his head,
Tapped another beer,
And slipped his arm around X.

2

Chicken Man sat, third row
from the back, aisle seat—
With a pistol shoved inside his pants.
("Lock! One magazine: Load!
Ready on the right! Ready on the left!
    The range is no longer clear!
    . . . At my command . . .")
Chicken Man slid up behind
Ms. Smiles and stuck
The pistol in her back
As he stared at the nape
Of her lovely neck
 . . . And thought of:
        Victor Charlie,
        With Gran Canyon
        Plowed in his nape
        by Mike Sixteen

        On Auto-Git-Um, Done-Got-Um.
("No Brass—No Ammo. Sir!
No grass—No acid, Sir!

Blood-Gore-On me, Sir!
—What do I do with it, Sir?'')

3

The SSS Troops
Sat with their wrinkles
In basements—
Everytown, USA;
When Chicken Man
Came home to roost.

He flapped his sleeveless arms
In each astonished face—
Fast screwing up
From the stench,
Cultivated in wet
Monsoon nights under a poncho.
He shook his long, matted hair
In each twisted face
And screamed:
     "I won't go away!"

"But who are you?"
Inquired the SSS troops,
When they caught their breath.
"I'm the man
With the gun
Behind your seat in the clouds.
I'm the man:
U.S. stamped, certified trained,
Guaranteed kill ratio,
Sealed for delivery—
Down on that jungle floor!"
Chicken Man squawked
At the gaping SSS troops.
Then, he ran flapping

Out into the plastic jungle—
        Screaming:
            "Who am I?
            You don't know,
            But I gotcher gun
                            Sam!!"

An Accident

It was up there,
Twenty pounds
Of oily iron,
Before it suddenly
Fell free
And pounced on my hand.

The hand
Jerked away
(Too late)
From vicious
Gear teeth.
The gashed wounds
Were deep,
With very white edges,
Before the blood
Ran out and down
The oil blackened hand.

I looked at the hand,
Healthy and whole
Only a moment ago—
Smashed now.
Perhaps it would heal
In time,
But the accident was done.

Frank A. Cross, Jr.

* * *

I remember
Wounds of others,
Much more terrible.
How easily
We living things
Are wounded
As we move
Among our machines.

ROBERT DANA

At the Vietnam War Memorial, Washington, D.C.

Today, everything takes
the color of the sun. The air
is filed and fine with it;
the dead leaves, lumped
and molten; flattened grass
taking it like platinum;
the mall, the simple, bare
plan of a tree standing
clothed and sudden in its
clean, explicable light.

And across the muddy
grounds of Constitution
Gardens, we've come to find
your brother's name, etched
in the long black muster
of sixteen years of war—
the earth walked raw
this morning by workmen still
gravelling paths, and people
brought here by dreams
more solemn than grief.

A kid in a sweater hurries
past us, face clenched
against tears. And couples,
grey-haired, touching hands,
their midwestern faces calm,
plain as the stencilled names

ranked on the black marble
in order of casualty.
The 57,939 dead. Soldiers,
bag-boys, lost insurance
salesmen, low riders
to nowhere gone no place—
file after broken file
of this army standing at rest.

Were there roses? I can't
remember. I remember
your son playing in the sun,
light as a seed. Beside
him, the names of the dead
afloat in the darker light
of polished stone. Reo
Owens. Willie Lee Baker.
Your brother. The names
of those who believed and
those who didn't, who died
with a curse on their lips
for the mud, the pitiless sea,
mists of gasoline and rain.

In your photograph, it's
1967. June. On the pad
of a carrier, Donald squats
in fatigues, smoking, beside
a rescue chopper, a man
loneliness kept lean;
the sea behind him slurs
like waste metal. He looks
directly at the camera, and
his eyes offer the serious
light of one who's folded
the empty hands of his
life once too often.
Before nightfall, his bird

CARRYING THE DARKNESS

will go down aslant God's
gaze like a shattered
grasshopper, and the moons
in the rice-paddies cry
out in burning tongues.

All words are obscene
beside these names. In the
morning the polished stone
gives back, we see ourselves—
two men, a woman, a boy,
reflected in grey light,
a dying world among the dead,
the dead among the living.
Down the poisoned Chesapeake,
leaking freighters haul
salt or chemicals. In a grey
room, a child rises in her
soiled slip and pops the
shade on another day; blue,
streaked with high cloud.

These lives once theirs
are now ours. The silver
air whistles into our lungs.
And underfoot, the world
lurches toward noon and
anarchy,—a future bright
with the vision of that
inconceivable, final fire-storm,
in which, for one dead second,
we shout our names, cut
them, like these, into air
deeper than any natural
shadow, darker than avenues
memoried in hidden trees.

STEVE DENNING

Kim-San

She is carried in with half her buttocks gone—
shrapnel close to her femoral nerve.
We tease the fragments out, flush the wound with
betadine and peroxide, turn a skin flap from her thigh
to cover the bare femur.

For two months she lies on her belly, the odor
of penicillin and infection in the sheets.
Slowly she learns English, learns our names
and where we came from, learns new words for stupor
and pain. We call her Kim-San;
she will be our interpreter.

Afternoons Kim-San sweeps the Captain's hooch,
washes his clothes in two buckets set on a wood ledge.
Before her wound heals, before she can sit,
she's pregnant.
The Captain props one leg in a stirrup
and scrapes the growth from her.
The next night Kim-San lies down beside him,
pulls the pin from a grenade.

We can't put the fire out, or won't, the sky
too thick to accept the stench.
We splash buckets of water over our tent to keep
flakes of burning canvas from spreading the fire.

In the morning we put them in body bags, take the
   Captain
to the airstrip, cover him with our flag.

Dau Tieng
South Vietnam 1968

Night on the Kho Bha Dinh

Two children move shells from Tay Ninh
to Dau Tieng on a water buffalo; one tugs the rein,
the other thumps the backbone with a small log.
In an M4-A Starlite Scope
I see them in and out of the infrared bush.
If I send up a flare, they'll be gone,
lost to the treeline, buffalo left grazing.

I fire on them—
tracers carom off the ground, the buffalo
spasms.

By morning the carcass has bloated,
eyes fly-bitten. In the gunnysacks
bananas we won't eat, cautious
of our own skins.

The Movie

We traded six AK-47s
for three air conditioners—
it was a steal—
traded two air conditioners
for a projector and screen

and a John Wayne western was thrown in,
and just when John's gettin' pissed,
just when he's about to ride into it all
the Cong loft mortars into camp
rip that screen
and I'm flat on my ass kicking the board floor
makin' it for the hole before another round
blows the boards and chairs apart.

"Wicklund."
"Where's Wicklund!"
Jesus, I'm in this hole and Wicklund's
out there bleeding from an artery in his neck,
shrapnel the size of a golf ball under his skin
and the mortars keep comin' and I'm scared
when I pick his loose body up

no pulse, wide pupils
only one thing makes any sense
run back pick up another
then another
and another

Fire Support Burk

1. The Siege

for two nights
the Cong overrun our wire
our 50 calibers, our teargas—
claymores rip them, still
some break through screaming

      N'ai
     N'ai
    N'ai

* * *

we press deep to the earth—
they circle,
run through again

    N'ai Chin
    N'ai Chin

we shout our names, can't tell
in the strikes of small-arm fire who
is who, who's left inside,
who's running
we shout our names
and fire
and fire
can't see who
    at who
    N'ai Chin
    N'ai Chin

2. Morning

half are women, some
girls with woven satchels
snared in the wire,
some as far as the treeline
shot with a single round
in the field others
opened as if a shock from inside
blew the lung through the rib.
Houser is dead,
Caudwell,
Sierra—loosened from his hole
he must have run with the Cong
as far as the riverbank, his head
under water.

This Time

we had 'em
had 'em in a crossfire, a platoon
of charlies caught sneakin'
from Chien Ly 5
ambushed 'em crossin' the river Li
watched 'em float

CEASE FIRE!
but Lip keeps poppin', runnin'
bush to bush like he's after somethin'
just not there, firing into tin
and straw, shoots a dead woman
shoots the ground around her, turns his weapon
on us, looks at us
but doesn't see
standin' there
not knowin'
and we're standin'
what to do
Lip fires on us

Gus wastes him
hits him clean

Lip's dead
and we're standin' round, someone's
talkin' to him as if he's alive
tellin' him he's goin' home
gettin' out
helps him up
dusts him off

W. D. EHRHART

Farmer Nguyen

When we swept through farmer Nguyen's hamlet,
some people said that farmer Nguyen
had given rice to the Vietcong.

  You picked the wrong side, farmer Nguyen.
  We took you in, and beat you,
  and put you in a barbed wire cage.

When the Vietcong returned to farmer Nguyen's
  hamlet,
some people said that farmer Nguyen
had given information to the Round Eyes.

  Wrong again, farmer Nguyen.
  They took more rice, and beat you,
  and made you carry supplies.

The One That Died

You bet we'll soon forget the one that died;
he isn't welcome any more.
He could too easily take our place
for us to think about him
any longer than it takes
to sort his personal effects:
    a pack of letters,

cigarettes,
photos and a wallet.
We'll keep the cigarettes;
divide them up among us.
His parents have no use for them,
and cigarettes are hard to get.

Night Patrol

Another night coats the nose and ears:
smells of fish and paddy water,
smoke from cooking fires and stale urine
drift uneasily, cloaked in silence;
the marketplace deserted, shuttered
houses, empty paths, all cloaked in silence;
shadows bristle.

Our gravel-crunching boots tear great
holes in the darkness, make us wince
with every step. A mangy dog
pits the stomach: rifles level;
nervous fingers hit the safety catch.

Guerrilla War

It's practically impossible
to tell civilians
from the Vietcong.

Nobody wears uniforms.
They all talk
the same language,

(and you couldn't understand them
even if they didn't).

They tape grenades
inside their clothes,
and carry satchel charges
in their market baskets.

Even their women fight;
and young boys,
and girls.

It's practically impossible
to tell civilians
from the Vietcong;

after a while,
you quit trying.

Time on Target

We used to get intelligence reports
from the Vietnamese district offices.
Every night, I'd make a list
of targets for artillery to hit.

It used to give me quite a kick
to know that I, a corporal,
could command an entire battery
to fire anywhere I said.

One day, while on patrol,
we passed the ruins of a house;
beside it sat a woman
with her left hand torn away;
beside her lay a child, dead.

* * *

When I got back to base,
I told the fellows in the COC;
it gave us all a lift to know
all those shells we fired every night
were hitting something.

Hunting

Sighting down the long black barrel,
I wait till front and rear sights
form a perfect line on his body,
then slowly squeeze the trigger.

The thought occurs
that I have never hunted anything in my whole life
except other men.

But I have learned by now
where such thoughts lead,
and soon pass on
to chow, and sleep,
and how much longer till I change my socks.

A Relative Thing

We are the ones you sent to fight a war
you didn't know a thing about.

It didn't take us long to realize
the only land that we controlled
was covered by the bottoms of our boots.

* * *

When the newsmen said that naval ships
had shelled a VC staging point,
we saw a breastless woman
and her stillborn child.

We laughed at old men stumbling
in the dust in frenzied terror
to avoid our three-ton trucks.

We fought outnumbered in Hue City
while the ARVN soldiers looted bodies
in the safety of the rear.
The cookies from the wives of Local 104
did not soften our awareness.

We have seen the pacified supporters
of the Saigon government
sitting in their jampacked cardboard towns,
their wasted hands placed limply in their laps,
their empty bellies waiting for the rice
some district chief has sold
for profit to the Vietcong.

We have been Democracy on Zippo raids,
burning houses to the ground,
driving eager amtracs through new-sown fields.

We are the ones who have to live
with the memory that we were the instruments
of your pigeon-breasted fantasies.
We are inextricable accomplices
in this travesty of dreams:
but we are not alone.

We are the ones you sent to fight a war
you did not know a thing about—
those of us that lived
have tried to tell you what went wrong.
Now you think you do not have to listen.

* * *

Just because we will not fit
into the uniforms of photographs
of you at twenty-one
does not mean you can disown us.

We are your sons, America,
and you cannot change that.
When you awake,
we will still be here.

Making the Children Behave

Do they think of me now
in those strange Asian villages
where nothing ever seemed
quite human
but myself
and my few grim friends
moving through them
hunched
in lines?

When they tell stories to their children
of the evil
that awaits misbehavior,
is it me they conjure?

To Those Who Have Gone
Home Tired

After the streets fall silent
After the bruises and the tear-gassed eyes are healed

After the consensus has returned
After the memories of Kent and My Lai and Hiroshima
lose their power
and their connections with each other
and the sweaters labeled Made in Taiwan
After the last American dies in Canada
and the last Korean in prison
and the last Indian at Pine Ridge
After the last whale is emptied from the sea
and the last leopard emptied from its skin
and the last drop of blood refined by Exxon
After the last iron door clangs shut
behind the last conscience
and the last loaf of bread is hammered into bullets
and the bullets
scattered among the hungry

What answers will you find
What armor will protect you
when your children ask you

Why?

Letter

to a North Vietnamese soldier
whose life crossed paths with mine
in Hue City, February 5th, 1968

Thought you killed me
with that rocket? Well, you nearly did:
splattered walls and splintered air,
knocked me cold and full of holes,
and brought the roof down on my head.

* * *

But I lived,
long enough to wonder often
how you missed; long enough
to wish too many times
you hadn't.

What's it like back there?
It's all behind us here;
and after all those years of possibility,
things are back to normal.
We just had a special birthday,
and we've found again our inspiration
by recalling where we came from
and forgetting where we've been.

Oh, we're still haggling over pieces
of the lives sticking out
beyond the margins of our latest
history books—but no one haggles
with the authors.

Do better than that
you cockeyed gunner with the brass
to send me back alive among a people
I can never feel
at ease with anymore:

remember where you've been, and why.
And then build houses; build villages,
dikes and schools, songs
and children in that green land
I blackened with my shadow
and the shadow of my flag.

Remember Ho Chi Minh
was a poet: please,
do not let it all come down
to nothing.

A Confirmation

for Gerry Gaffney

Solemn Douglas firs stride slowly
down steep hills to drink
the waters of the wild Upper Umqua.
In a small clearing in the small
carved ravine of a feeder stream
we camp, pitching our tent
in the perfect stillness of the shadows
of the Klamath Indians. Far off,
almost in a dream, the logging trucks
growl west down through the mountains
toward the mills in Roseburg.

I hold the stakes, you hammer:
"Watch the fingers!"—both laughing.
Both recall, in easy conversation,
one-man poncho-tents rigged
side by side in total darkness,
always you and I, in iron heat,
in the iron monsoon rains—
not like this at all; and yet,
though years have passed
and we are older by a lifetime,
a simple slip of thought, a pause,
and here: nothing's changed.

For we were never young, it seems;
not then, or ever. I couldn't even cry
the day you went down screaming, angry
jagged steel imbedded in your knee—
I knew you would live,
and I knew you wouldn't be back,

and I was glad, and a little jealous.
Two months later I went down.

We all went down eventually,
the villages aflame, the long
grim lines of soldiers, flotsam
in the vortex of a sinking illusion:
goodbye, Ginny; goodbye, John Kennedy;
goodbye, Tom Paine and high school history—
though here we are still, you and I.
We live our lives now
in a kind of awkward silence
in the perfect stillness of the shadows
of the Klamath Indians.

And I am truly happy
to be with you again. We stand
on the rocks; you point to clear
patches between white water
where the shadows of sleek fish slip,
effortless streaks of energy.
I'm clumsy: with an old, eager patience
you teach me how to cast the fly
gently, so it rides on the surface
with the current, far downstream—
till the rod bends, springs back,
bends again: strike! Your excitement
rises above the river like a wild
song the Douglas firs bend
imperceptibly to hear: shouts,
advice, encouragement, half an hour
and a fourteen-inch rainbow trout
panting hard, eyes alive, its tiny heart
beating with defiance still unbroken
though I hold the fish
helpless in my hands.

I throw the fish back
in the awkward silence, and you

slip your arm around my shoulders
gently for a moment, knowing why.

Later we eat from cans,
the rainbow flashing in the fire
reflecting in our eyes, alive:
familiar gestures—fingers burned
by hot tin lids, a mild curse, quiet
laughter, swish of a knifeblade
plunging idly deep into damp earth.
You ask do I remember the little shy
flower who always wore a white ao dai,
and I smile across the flames as the river
tumbles through the darkness toward the sea
that laps the shores of Asia.

The wind moves through the Douglas firs,
and in the perfect stillness of the shadows
of the Klamath Indians, we test
our bonds and find them, after all
these years, still sound—knowing
in the awkward silence we will always share
something worth clinging to
out of the permanent past of stillborn dreams:
the ancient, implacable wisdom
of ignorance shattered forever, a new
reverence we were never taught
by anyone we believed, a frail hope
we gave each other, communion
made holy by our shame.

You've found religion since then,
a wife, and two children;
I write poems you admire.
The knee's still stiff, like an old
high school football wound,
and I have trouble hearing. We are
both tired, but reluctant to sleep:
both understand we will never

see each other again; once is enough.
The logging trucks have long since
left the mountains in peace;
in the perfect stillness, we can almost
hear the solemn Douglas firs drinking
the waters of the wild Upper Umqua
we have come so far to worship:
together now, in this small circle of light,
we bow our hearts to the shadows
of the Klamath Indians; now,
and always, in our need.

The Invasion of Grenada

I didn't want a monument,
not even one as sober as that
vast black wall of broken lives.
I didn't want a postage stamp.
I didn't want a road beside the Delaware
River with a sign proclaiming:
"Vietnam Veterans Memorial Highway."

What I wanted was a simple recognition
of the limits of our power as a nation
to inflict our will on others.
What I wanted was an understanding
that the world is neither black-and-white
nor ours.

What I wanted
was an end to monuments.

The Blizzard of Sixty-Six

Snow came early here, and hard:
roads treacherous; wires down.
School authorities should have cancelled
the annual high school Christmas dance:
two couples died on the way home.
"Tragedy," the local papers declared,
but the snow kept falling.

Somewhere in a folder in a file
is a photograph of me in a uniform:
one stripe for PFC; girl in a yellow gown.
I took her home through the falling snow,
kissed goodnight, and left for Asia.

All through that long year, snow
fell and fell on the green rice,
on gray buffalo, thatched huts, green
patrols, and the mounting yellow dead.

Randy, class of '65, died
in terminal cold in the Mekong Delta;
Kenny, class of '66, died in a blizzard
of lead in the Central Highlands;
I came home with permanent chills,
the yellow nameless dead of Asia
crammed into my seabag, and all of us
looking for a reason.

We never found one. Presidents
come and go away like snowdrifts
in driveways; generals come and go;
the earth goes on silently turning

and turning through its seasons,
and the snow keeps falling.

". . . the light that cannot fade . . ."

Suzie, you picked a hell of a time
to teach me about mortality.
I was in North Carolina then,
talking tough, eating from cans,
wearing my helmet John Wayne style—
and you were suddenly dead:
a crushed skull on a pre-dawn road
just two weeks shy of college,
and me about to leave for Vietnam.

I wanted you and me alive;
I wanted out.
That night I cried till dawn.

Funny, how I managed to survive
that war, how the years have passed,
how I'm thirty-four and getting on,
and how your death
bestowed upon my life a permanence
I never would have had
if you had lived:

you'd have gone to college,
married some good man from Illinois,
and disappeared like all the other
friends I had back then who meant
so much and whom I haven't
thought about in years.

But as it is, I think of you
whenever dancers flow across a stage

or graceful gymnasts balance on the beam.
And every time I think of you,
you're young.

for Carolyn Sue Brenner, 1948–1966

CHARLES FISHMAN

Death March

Not the numbers   but the sound—
murmurs in the single-file crowds
flickering windy candles,
not the place   but the names
marked on placards hung
from living necks—
to be tolled to the cameras
for a visual kaddish,
not the hour   but the clear darkness
through which mourners   like monks
in 14th-century habits   passed the shrine—
the great doomed Capitol
Taj Mahal
sepulchre of the dead Prince: Justice.

Each of us one of the silent dead
returned to march through the white city
past white TV lamps holding white candles
past the White House in our white bones,
a parade of resurrected soldiers—
bearers of ghost guns and phantom armor
decked with blood medals and chevrons of flesh
garlanded with the black hungers
of our enemies—
camouflaged as war protesters
bearing our constitutional
wounds.

BRYAN ALEC FLOYD

Private Ian Godwin, U.S.M.C.

He stepped on a land mine,
falling up instead of down.
Afterward he lay still, listening
to his feet get up without him
and slowly walk away.
For this he was given a medal,
which he swallowed.
He was given crutches,
which he burned.
Flown Med-Evac to San Diego,
he was ordered to rehabilitate.
But he started to salute bedpans
and give orders to hypos,
and tell catheters to "Fire!"
He stood on his stumps,
yelling that he was going
to chase daisies up the hills
because winter had greened into spring,
that God had become rain and it was raining,
the soft mud of Vietnam cool between his toes.

Sergeant Brandon Just, U.S.M.C.

He was alive with death:
Her name was Sung
and she was six years old.

By slightest mistake of degrees
on an artillery azimuth,
he had called for rockets and napalm.
Their wild wizardry of firepower
expired her mistake of a village,
killing everyone except her,
and napalm made her look
like she was dead among the dead,
she alone alive among their upturned corpses
burning toward the sky.
He and the platoon
got to them too late,
removing only her
to a hospital inside his base, Da Nang.
In the months that followed,
when he could make it back from the boonies,
he always went to visit Sung.
Finally he was ordered to a desk job at the base.
He visited her every day,
though he accused himself of being alive
and would stand in a slump,
breathing his despair,
before entering the children's ward.
But he would enter.
Sung, knowing it was him,
would turn toward the sound of his feet,
her own, seared beyond being feet,
crisply trying to stand on shadows,
cool but unseen.
And as he would come in,
Sung would hobble up to him
in her therapeutic cart,
smiling even when she did not smile, lipless,
her chin melted to her chest
that would never become breasts.
He would stand
and wait for her touch upon his hand
with her burn-splayed fingers

that came to lay a fire upon his flesh.
Sung was alive
and would live on despite life,
but even now her skull
seemed to be working its way through
the thin, fragile solids of wasted, waxen skin.
Her head was as bald as a bomb
whose paint had peeled.
She had no nose
and her ears were gone.
Her eyes had been removed,
and because they were not there,
they were there
invisibly looking him through.
Sung was child-happy
that he came and cared,
and when he would start to leave,
she would agonize her words
out of the hollow that was her mouth.
Her tongue, bitten in two while she had burned,
strafing his ears,
saying, without mercy,
I love you.

Corporal Charles Chungtu, U.S.M.C.

This is what the war ended up being about:
we would find a V.C. village,
and if we could not capture it
or clear it of Cong,
we called for jets.
The jets would come in, low and terrible,
sweeping down, and screaming,
in their first pass over the village.
Then they would return, dropping their first bombs

that flattened the huts to rubble and debris.
And then the jets would sweep back again
and drop more bombs
that blew the rubble and debris
to dust and ashes.
And then the jets would come back once again,
in a last pass, this time to drop napalm
that burned the dust and ashes to just nothing.
Then the village
that was not a village any more
was our village.

Lance Corporal Purdue Grace, U.S.M.C.

He went home when the new replacements arrived,
but before he left
he talked with several of them,
all of whom looked scared and a bit self-pitying.
They knew he had made it through his tour
without getting a cold much less a wound.
One of the braver replacements
told him they were all terrified.
The Lance Corporal told them, "To be scared is okay.
I've seen lots of men change their pants
more than once a day, they were so scared.
But don't expect sympathy.
Sympathy is a sad word found in the dictionary
somewhere between scab and syphilis.
Always remember to keep your head out of your ass
and your ass out of the air.
Know this about this fucked-up war
that will never unfuck itself—
Life in Vietnam is a sea of shit:
Some people sink.

Some people swim.
And some people go in boats."

Private Jack Smith, U.S.M.C.

Since he came back
he never met with the friends he fought with in Nam
and never mentioned the war:
Once he was ordered out
of his five-man fire team
to go and be point man.
He was about a hundred feet up front
when someone in his fire team
tripped a land mine,
and whoever it had been,
along with the other three,
were left somehow
unreasonably alive—just.
And there had been a Lance Corporal in his squad
whom the threat of peace always made aggressive.
The Lance Corporal was a sniper
with twenty-six kills marked up.
The Private was with him
when the Lance Corporal was cut down by a V.C.
    sniper,
and as the Private held him,
the Lance Corporal held his intestines in his hands,
saying, "I don't want to die. I'm afraid to die."
And died.
One night the Private and two other guys
slept in a sandbagged hootch
that was hit by two direct mortar rounds,
he being blasted awake and away
without a scratch
while those other two

were just pieces of themselves.
He could not find their heads
but laid the rest to rest
in ponchos that no one could tag
because their remains were Officially Unidentifiable.
After that he decided
to avoid moderation at any extreme
and shot every anything that moved.
He came to think that his officers
were more concerned with rank and medals
than with the lives and deaths of their men.
He came to feel that his politicians were garbage
who should have been wasted.
When he finished his tour of duty
and was sent home and Honorably Discharged,
he decided to live with his parents
and began college,
and majored in History on the GI Bill.
He thought he might join the peace movement
and started going to rallies.
His college was shut down four times
the semester he started,
and during the fourth shutdown,
his college president was beaten up
by several anti-imperialists
who took over the college
and burned down the ROTC building
and the library
and who kept the president in his office
until he resigned, on his own accord of course.
But the ex-Private kept going to the rallies,
looked, listened, learned.
He got to thinking
that most of the rally speakers
were happy with hallucinations,
and he thought
that several of the tens of thousands
in the crowds who kept yelling Right On

had either forgotten, or had never known,
that absolutism is addictive
and that the mob, any mob for any cause,
is always
pregnant with fascism.
The fifth time his college was shut down
by the anti-imperialist anti-
fascists,
he knew what he knew,
and knew that he must try
to walk through and beyond the mob
which had blocked his way to History.
He tried, knowing they would beat hell out of him,
and they did.
But it was he who was arrested
for disturbing the peace.
He was jailed.
His dad bailed him out
and told him he hoped he was satisfied
and that he should have felt ashamed.
But instead, the ex-Private felt himself feel nothing.
He went home again, and packed, and left.
That was four years ago.
Nobody has heard from him since.

Captain James Leson, U.S.M.C.

His corpse was returned
to the U.S. in March, 1974, from Hanoi,
where the criminal Captain had been
a prisoner from 1967 until his natural death in 1973.
An official spokesman
of the Peoples' Republic of North Vietnam
related with regrets
that the bourgeois elitist officer

had confessed to having been a lackey
for the war-mongering capitalists
and their running dogs, the South Vietnamese.
The official spokesman said
the aristocratic officer, without being intimidated,
had confessed that he had enjoyed killing innocent
    children
and had loved watching cities and villages burn.
And that before the imperialist Captain had naturally
    died,
he had written his regrets and spoken them over the
    radio
that his sins and the sins of his mafia nation
could have been avoided
had he been as brave as a Rennie Davis or a Jane Fonda
and his country as committed to fighting inequality and
    racism
as the governments of Sweden and India.
Enough said,
he said before he died his natural death.

Corporal Kevin Spina, U.S.M.C.

He came of a sharecrop farm family
and could barely read and write.
He had never thought
about teaching his heart war.
When he personally received
a letter from the President
of the United States of America
he simply went, having faith.
He put on his uniform
and disappeared
and became his uniform.
When he came back in a box,

he was buried with full military honors,
his family given the flag
that draped his coffin.
Now that flag flies every day
in front of his house.
When the neighbors' children pass by
they always look at that flag
and they always say,
"Someday there will be another war,
and I'm going to be a Marine."

Private First Class Brooks Morgenstein, U.S.M.C.

Her remembered frailty had strengthened his.
His soul was alive for her.
What kept him going
when he would bag and tag bodies
or when out on a search-and-destroy
were her eyes as soft as breasts.
He wanted to write his wife naked words
that would have been more naked when read.
He had chosen the goal of his groin
and it was to grieve,
for his want of her was like pain.
His loneliness and lust were his and he theirs
during every second of these thirteen months.
He only knew as he held his rifle
during a sweeping operation
that next year he would hold her,
and when he kissed her,
his tongue would touch hers
and she would feel
as though a piece of the sun
was in her mouth.

When someone in his platoon
was sent back in pieces, alive or dead,
he tried not to despair of heaven,
but sometimes he had faith only in flesh
and would think of her thighs
and remember God.
The heat of the jungle
had pared him thin as peace.
His head was shaven squabby bald.
His uniform clung to him like a huge wet sock,
and he stank of leeches and mud and malaria and fear.
Yet he was all he had,
and his heart would leave him, and long to her heart,
she who had been shy to yield, but had yielded.
The sun in the boonies gloomed everything
with its yellowed heat for air,
but he breathed her fingers.
And her young woman's youngest breasts
suckled his terror,
while her mouth held off boredom
from shattering him insane.
Under a rocket barrage at Khe Sanh,
he once dreamed of her lying open as a wound,
and as raw,
and he had salved and bandaged her
with his mouth and fingers.
During the bad times,
such as when the platoon was ordered to torch a
    village,
he would feel his rage deepening,
without bottoming out,
and he would be shaking with fear and shame and
    ecstasy
that he was still alive.
He would make himself think of her,
and with the thirst that comes from drinking of it,
his lust would grow and become exalted
like a great tree,

and he knew if he made it back
she could climb his body
and that he with branches would cover her with himself
and they would be unable to tell
how much of him was him
and how much of him was her.

DAVID HALL

Disgrace

If Juan Rodriguez is alive today
I'd like to tell him that
to step on a mine
your first step into war

is no disgrace.

What will my mother say?
he asked the medics
bending over him
knowing he shouldn't see
what all he'd lost.

What will she think
of her clumsy son?

I'd like to say
I've seen good men
take longer,
long enough to think
their country putrefied:

I knew one boy
who ate gunpowder
and died.

I'd like to say
I've seen men cry

and try to swat the bullets
away like bees

and watched one young man
tired of dying
shoot off both his knees.

I huddled half my year in mud
and couldn't remember my mother's face—

believe me Juan
your friends who stayed
went far beyond disgrace.

Excerpts from "The Ambush of the Fourth Platoon"

2
There is no place to hide
this day or any other.
By dawn the wide sky
already clotted with great grey clouds
that rumble and bump each other
like fat men on a subway
back home
back home
splits open at one invisible seam
to let through the angels
of our doom: the helicopters
come to lift us
so many in one short day
to paradise.

4
How is it the stomach knows first
before the heart can demand forgiveness

before the brain can wake
to coax us under a cot?
Later this day the stomach will clench
around its last metallic meal
and the muscles
which ought to be churning
after footballs
will twitch in place
as in a bad dream
when no amount of running
makes things move.

5

How strange to come down
in mud
so far from home.
How strange to hear nothing
but the sloshing of our boots in mud
the clatter of angels
scattering on the wind.

6

I should have seen this land
when blood stayed in its place
in the veins of the people.
I should have seen the temples
intact
the families dancing after the harvest;
I should have seen myself
shattered
in the mirrors of the fields
and stayed where I belonged.

7

Mothers and fathers of the West:
these are not soldiers;
these are your sons
in dirty uniforms.

The soldiers here all pray
to different gods. In the jungle
the Viet Cong take root
like palms
like sticky ferns
like weeds in the garden
of our innocence.

8

We stop at the edge of knee-deep water
while all around the rice plants quiver
in a breeze we can't detect.
In my father's war
the young men knew who was wrong
and blazed into death
with clear consciences.
Here
under monsoon clouds
it is grey all over
and no one looks guilty
but me.

9

Give us this day
a plane ticket back to San Francisco;
give us another chance
to size things up
just one more low-pitched whine
before the draft board.
Give us a cigarette or two
a slug from somebody's
spiked canteen.

10

The mind could stretch out here
like a python
savoring one last meal.
But listen: everywhere

behind this green curtain
rifles cock—
O Jesus
I have the gold pins to prove
I went to all that Sunday School.
O Mother
it's time to turn
your head.

11

All around me
young men squeal
like children fallen
on a gravel playground.

12

From the ferns they emerge
like awful butterflies
from the earth's cocoon.
The spoils go quickly:
the watch some girlfriend gave
for luck
is carefully unstrapped;
the ring a grandfather handed down goes
finger and all.
And who is this coming to call on me?
There is fish on his breath
as he leans above me.

13

I have moved to the suburbs
of consciousness
where the racket my friends make
as they suffer
seems just a city job
left behind.
I have never heard anyone die
in a Brooklyn accent.

Somewhere
someone is shooting
someone in the head.
Above
the storm clouds loosen
and soon the warm rain
will wash my face clean.

14

I combed my hair in ducktails
in that eighth grade history class
when Mrs. Porter said God would never allow
the Communists domination over
a Christian people
and Mrs. Porter
this day
grows old and fat
on her porch back home
unmolested
by the yellow horde
and if my gold pins mean anything
Mrs. Porter
expect a rattling of your windows
some terrible night:
we have much to discuss
and we both have much
to learn.

GUSTAV HASFORD

Bedtime Story

Sleep, America.
Silence is a warm bed.
Sleep your nightmares of small
    cries cut open now
    in the secret places of
Black Land, Bamboo City.

Sleep tight, America
    dogtags eating sweatgrimaced
    TV-people
Five O'clock news: My son the Meat.

Laughing scars, huh?
    Novocained fist.
Squeeze every window empty
    then hum.

Fear only the natural unreality
    and kiss nostalgia goodbye
Bayonet teddy bear and snore.
Bad dreams are something you ate.
    So sleep, you mother.

STEVE HASSETT

Mother's Day

Staring at the almost
nonexistent tits of the first
teenage girl we'd ever seen
in a vill, Green
grabs his balls and
makes obscene noises
gramma gums a smile
nodding her head dumbly
while little brother gets
a taste of pre-sweetened
koolade from R.J.'s canteen
two women beat feet
to the well and back
with tin buckets but
too slow . . . the thatch
is dry and half the roof
by now is up in flames.

Sin loi, mama-san,
we burnin your hootch
battalion says you v.c.

Armed Forces Day

We fuckin never had a fuckin chance
halfway up that useless fuckin hill

we hit the shit an lost the doc
the RTO an all three goddam
squad leaders and two platoons
got pretty chewed up trying to
make the ridge but no one can say
the men of Alpha company didn't
make one goddam good effort up
on that hill and I'm sure
that, even after we had to fly in
another battalion, my men
will agree in my saying that charley
gave us one hell of a fight but
there was never any doubt and the feeling
here at brigade is that while our
casualties were heavier than we'd
have liked them to be, the overall
kill-ratio is highly in our favor in
light of the gains made, division
TOC announced today, the outcome
has been entirely satisfactory with the
hill, a fortified enemy stronghold, taken
late Tuesday after three days of assaults
made by elements of two battalions
which received light to moderate losses,
USARV's spokesman said, during the course
of the operation in which a force
of NVA regulars was trapped on
Hill 618 on the Cambodian border
was abandoned today according to
the Department of Defense briefing
only one week after elements of a
US airborne division spent
four days securing it.

Thanksgiving

Nothing, not even victory
will erase the terrible hole of blood:
nothing, neither the sea, nor the passing
of sand and time, nor the geranium burning
over the grave.

PABLO NERUDA

By the third day, the rain
drills imprecise circles in
our faces, undermines the shoulders,
curses in every oriental
tongue, transforms the blood in-
to water, sharpens the mud:
the rain drips from every leaf
and vine, flows from the arms like
hatred, turns legs to butter,
augurs to the leeches, sheaths
the feet in pyramids of mud:
the rain blooms on the slopes
of our fingers, whispers of the
passing of departed arks, crumples
their justifications in
cupped hands like a cigarette,
kept dry these three days under
the helmet, shredding
by the second drag:
the earth becomes our greatest enemy.

Next day the maps tell lies.
The radios can only gag. Rain
falls like ice detached from
time. Each drop severs minutes

from our lives and sets them free,
like grains of rice. Each grain
contains a sea and every shore
one footprint. No patrol
has ever been this lost. Streams ignore
the dictates of the land. Their
current sweeps away two men:
rocks strip them into newsprint
and maptacks. No rations left.
No water fit to drink. Vines dance
in delirium. The mud goes mad.
Day ends like the dimming
of lights opposite a death-row
cell. Night spreads like ants across
the carcass of a water buffalo.

Dead before dawn, eyeless:
exhausted and betrayed by sleep.
No holes dug. No one on guard.
Our ammo caked with mud. Nothing
takes us on. Dice stuck to its hand
with blood, morning curses, coughs
and spits the sun. Like malaria
from a patient, we raise battalion
through its static shroud.
We are the litter of fear, the sur-
vivors of envy. The misery
that builds cities goes with
the rain. Deep wells of bitterness
remain. Fire failed,
we store water against the day
you will dance us to the edge
of our grave. Do you think you buy
our future with resupply? Thanks
anyway for rations and dry socks
but whatever happened to Washington
across the Delaware,
Custer's dying to the Sioux,
VE Day,

or Dien Bien Phu to the enemy
we can't find for you?

Christmas

The Hessian in his last letter home
said in part

"they are all rebels here
who will not stand to fight
but each time fade before us
as water into sand . . .

the children beg in their rude hamlets

the women stare with hate

the men flee into the barrens at our approach
to lay in ambush

some talk of desertion . . .
were it not for the hatred
they bear us, more would do so

There is no glory here.
Tell Hals he must evade the Prince's levy
through exile or deformity

Winter is hard upon us. On the morrow we enter
Trenton. There we rest till the New Year. . . .

Steve Hassett

Patriot's Day

When the young girls rolled into one
and she without a face became
death's ikon,
    and to the silence of our fathers
seemed to offer as redemption Vietnam,
we went.

Now we bring our dead to supper.

All our women are warriors
and the men burn slowly inward.

• • •

And what would you do, ma,
if eight of your sons step
out of the TV and begin
killing chickens and burning
hooches in the living room,
stepping on booby traps
and dying in the kitchen,
beating your husband and
taking him and shooting
skag and forgetting in
the bathroom?

would you lock up your daughter?
would you stash the apple pie?
would you change channels?

SAMUEL HAZO

Battle News

For breakfast—war and coffee. Pilots
have been downed like skeet, and captives
tortured in a tub or booted in the groin
until they talked. A Cardinal approves
of troop morale. His speech before

the V.F.W. is reproduced beneath
the photo of a sergeant burned in error.
After three wars, I should be numb
to every morning's muster of the dead.
The Cardinal seems numb enough. He preached

a twin address the year I swore
to fight all foreign and domestic
enemies with nothing but my hands, so help
me God. When I marched home, I might
have told his Eminence, "Don't

talk pluralities to me. I breathe
alone and so do you, and one
times one was never more than one.
The smallest pin of pain can show
that one umtillionth of the world

is not the name that anybody answers to."
I never breathed a word, and now the daily
deathcount booked between the weather

and the baseball scores leaves nothing new
to say. The cost remains numerical,

the order, alphabetical. Only the spellings
change from war to war. Between
the lines I think of aborigines
who would not touch their wives or eat
until they had atoned for every

enemy they speared in battle. Justice
or no justice, shall no one say
that hunters rove the earth from now
to heaven? Who cares if men in diving
suits are swimming to the moon like sperm?

They're out for battlefields where flying
armies shall dispute the stars. I know
it's militarily absurd to claim that life
means more than trying not to die,
but if it does, what then? What now?

GEORGE HITCHCOCK

Scattering Flowers

It is our best and prayerful judgment that they (air attacks) are a necessary part of the surest road to peace.

LYNDON B. JOHNSON

There is a dark tolling in the air,
an unbearable needle in the vein,
the horizon flaked with feathers of rust.
From the caves of drugged flowers
fireflies rise through the night:
they bear the sweet gospel of napalm.

Democracies of flame are declared
in the villages, the rice fields
seethe with blistered reeds.
Children stand somnolent on their crutches.
Freedom, a dancing girl,
lifts her petticoats of gasoline,
and on the hot sands of a deserted beach
a wild horse struggles, choking
in the noose of diplomacy.

Now in their cane chairs the old men
who listen for the bitter wind
of bullets, spread on their thighs
maps, portfolios, legends of hair,
and photographs of dark Asian youths
who are already dissolving into broken water.

DANIEL HOFFMAN

A Special Train

Banners! Bunting! The engine throbs
In waves of heat, a stifling glare
Tinges the observation-car

And there, leaning over the railing,
What am I
Doing in the Orient?

Blackflies, shrapnel-thick, make bullocks
Twitch. The peasants stand
Still as shrines,

And look, in this paddy
A little boy is putting in the shoots.
He's naked in the sunlight. It's my son!

There he is again, in that
Field where the earth-walls meet.
It's his play-time. See, his hands are smeared

With mud, and now his white
Back is flecked with ash, is seared
By embers dropping from the sky—

The train chuffs past. I cry
Stop! Stop! We cross another paddy,
He's there, he's fallen in the mud, he moans my name.

PETER HOLLENBECK

Anorexia

Something drained our blood and it wasn't the leeches
Something made us tired and it wasn't the lack of sleep
Something chilled us and it wasn't the rain
Grey, long-falling, whispering across the paddies
With the mountains in the distance,
Dark green in the distance,
Mountains in the rain.

Something made us shudder and it wasn't the vermin
Scuttling through the trenches,
The rats grown fat and bold, the cockroaches gliding
Across your boots, looking for mold,
As a radio played Herman's
Hermits, played the Beatles,
And something—not age—made us old.

Something hunted us and it wasn't the Cong
Relentless, pushing us further back
As it grew dark, low on ammo, the soles of our feet
Cheesy and white,
No, not the lean Cong, the mean Cong,
Behind us in the thorny vines,
Cutting off retreat.

Something seared us beyond the fire
That grew and twisted above the hootch's grey
    remains,
Hotter and brighter, it cut through the mists

Of reasons and arithmetic, piercing the common
   daylight;
There were times when all we could do was watch
The unfolding atrocity, observe, under the stern
   masters,
The civilized restraints disintegrate.

JOHN F. HOWE

The Land

The Vietcong are magical. They can see in darkness. At night you can watch them moving around in the bush. They are shadowy clumps crawling across the jungle floor, coming at you, creeping hunched over, bending low and floating in the dark haze of vegetation. Sometimes you can hear them, mostly not, and when you do they sound like owls and wind and falling rock.

The Vietcong are mystical. They turn to smoke and float over mountains. You kill them and they disappear. They crawl through rows of concertina and razor wire without making as much as a whisper. They can see everything and they know everything, even days before the rumors get to us. Where they know you will be going, they plant things in the ground along the trail that explode in loud orange and black CRACKS when you step on them, or things that go pop, real soft and fizzing like, when you trip on the wires that they string across the narrow footpaths. All of these things take your legs off, or your balls, or your hands, or other things that you need. The bigger ones are not so mean and degrading. They don't spare you anything, they just make you disappear.

The VC can swim for miles under water, and in the current look like floating reeds or patches of weed. They are haze in the morning, and distant rippling heat waves across a flat paddy in the afternoon. At night they are shadows that turn into bushes at first light.

Sexton says that they can do these things because they are the land. It is a philosophy, he says. They and the land are one and the same, and I nod because now I have an understanding and I nod again because I don't want to know anymore.

Once, on a sultry afternoon hump across the valley, we spotted four VC crossing an open expanse of brown checkerboard paddies. They were about seven hundred meters away and nearing a treeline at the far end of the basin. We waited for the lieutenant to make contact with Battalion and Sexton passed the binoculars along the crouching column. I had never seen a VC before. I leaned across the dike, resting the glasses on top of the packed earth. The heat rises in wavering chorus lines in the distance. They are walking in column, rifles slung casually across the sweat-stained backs of their tan khaki uniforms, and moving crisply. The one at the rear of the column turns, looking back across the flat, and I lower my eyes from the glasses, thinking he can see me.

CHRISTOPHER HOWELL

A Reminder to the Current President

for Lewis Cook, 1945–1969

On an average afternoon men lay down
rifles, leaning into heat
from which a few will not rise
again. "It is because of shrapnel,"
we say. "It is because of hatred
and ageless dispute and love
of country, which we have learned."
Though the cleanly young seem deathless
as this language passes over them,
neither the *zip* nor the sound of the plane
nor the singing wakes them.

On an average afternoon
by the trimmed shores, pacing, waiting
for news, the loved ones
approach the exact moment
which will not decode: a projector runs
on and on in a dark theater
and the doors are locked. A drumroll
circles the drillfield. Carbines
sound once, twice, and again. Who
will cast dirt down into the cool rest
of itself? Why does the film go on
showing and showing these few gathered
in sunlight around a space so empty
only the earth can fill it?

* * *

Questions. We are advised to let them ride.
We are advised that life continues.
That, on an average afternoon, the mother
will be given medals and a speech.
That all of this will be long ago,
like an unused wisdom.
"God's flag is our flag," it says
in the handbooks. "Therefore, be comforted
and clean of conscience: these deaths
are part of a plan." Meanwhile, the film
is rewinding; and the sound of a plane sails
the dimming heavens, far off, like a telegram
on its way.

Memories of Mess Duty and the War

Garbage went over the fantail, boiling into blue
white wake. Among shark snouts rising to sample that
sweetness, it rode like the raw
stuff of hope. We watched. Our aprons dripping.
Who knew what we, six hundred miles from shore,
thought? What we were doing there (the abstract
crime afloat) kept glittering
phosphor-like in the day to day, unnamed. We didn't
    guess
the sea of harm on which we moved. We smoked.
We missed our women in the glo-bake blackness
of the crew's compartment, hated brass, cursed
our uniforms and thought that was enough. Grinning,
thoughtless, the cargo burned at Asia. Let the garbage
    sink
then, let sharks sever bone from scrap
and keep on following. Still, on the floor,
our longings and the spilled blood
gathered.

Liberty & Ten Years of Return

for the veterans

1

In the singed breath of London
we were lost
and aching sailors burnt by ships.
Disgusted, lonely, broke we four
buddies went adrift, sealed
casks of withered lust. Above the dim
lamps our President kept saying "No.
We love a rigid chaos. Get laid
if you like, but nobody leaves."

2

A few cops passed like blue
trees moving. A taxi splashed dark
on our dark American frowns.
Hours we spoke of the trains, chanting,
mythical; of penalties
for missing muster, ship's movement,
the long glide home. At last, shivering
we stared down years of open windows
till the third-class cars pulled out
for Portsmouth in the teeth of dawn.

3

None of us expected this
arrival, the band strewn dead
on an empty pier, the fleet crusted
and opening like a bowl of dazed peonies
to the chalk sky. Now
we see: ours is an absent life, no healing.

Sent over the great sea
a decade has returned us with no riches,
no message, and no home waiting
or wanting us here.

DAVID HUDDLE

Nerves

Training I received did not apply be-
cause Cu Chi District was not Fort Jackson.
Funniest thing, they had dogs like any-
where, used them for sandwich meat, I ate one
once, but I guess you want to know if I
ever shot somebody—didn't—would have
—curious about it, but my job gave
one duty, to ask questions. I'd lie

if I said some weren't women, children,
old men; I'd lie too if I claimed my mem-
ories weren't part of my life, but then
shame is natural, wear it, every day
think of bursting from sleep when mortars came:
crazy run to a dark hole, damp sandbags.

Theory

Everybody dug a hole and lived in it
when Division first cleared the land near Cu Chi.
Snipers kept the men low a while, but then tents
went up, then big tents. Later, frames of wood, screen
wire siding, and plywood floors rose under those tents
and that was called a hooch. Time I got there,
base camp was five square miles of hooches, not
a sniper round was fired in daylight, and good posture

* * *

was common. What we wanted was a tin roof.
I was there the day we got the tin to do it with,
blistering hot even that morning we stripped off
the old canvas, took hammers and climbed the rafters
to nail down sheets of tin. Drinking beer afterwards,
we were the sweaty survivors, we were the fit.

Bac Ha

As G-5 put it, Bac Ha hamlet was a good
neighbor in 25th Infantry Division's
eyes. Neighbor was fact, eyes was a lie, and good
was a joke for a fool. Holes in the fence,
paths to the guard shacks, were for Bac Ha whores,
famous for clap, who maybe last year'd worn white
ao dais and ribboned hats to walk the warm
mornings to school, lessons from French-taught
     priests.

Division's garbage dump was three acres
fenced off from that hamlet's former front yard.
Black-toothed women, children, former farmers
squatted in the shade all day, smiled at the guards,
watched what the trucks dumped out. Walking nights
out there, you'd be under somebody's rifle sights.

Words

What did those girls say when you walked the strip
of tin shack bars, gewgaw stores, barber shops,
laundries and restaurants, most all of which
had beds in back, those girls who had to get up

in Saigon before dawn to catch their rides to Cu Chi,
packed ten to a Lambretta, chattering, gay
in their own lovely tongue, on the dusty
circus road to work, but then what did they say?

Come here, talk to me, you handsome, GI
I miss you, I love you too much, you want
short time, go in back, I don't care, I want
your baby, sorry about that, GI,
you number ten. A history away
I translate dumbly what those girls would say.

Cousin

for John H. Kent, Jr., 1919–1982

I grew up staring at the picture of him:
oak leaves on his shoulders, crossed rifles
on his lapels, and down his chest so many medals
the camera lost them. He wore gold-rimmed
glasses, smiled, had jokes to tell. World War Two
exploded for me summers on the front porch
when he'd visit and talk. Wounded twice, he knew
he'd almost died. Courage rang in his voice.

Ten years from my war, thirty from his, we
hit a summer visit together; again
the stories came. He remembered names of men,
weapons, tactics, places, and I could see
his better than mine. He'd known Hemingway!
I tried hard couldn't find a thing to say.

David Huddle

Vermont

I'm forty-one. I was twenty-three then.
I'm here with what I've dreamed or remembered.
In the Grand Hotel in Vung Tau one weekend
I spent some time with the most delicate
sixteen-year-old girl who ever delivered
casual heartbreak to a moon-eyed GI.
I am trying to make it balance, but I
can't. Believe me, I've weighed it out:

rising that morning up to the cool air where
the green land moved in its own dream down there,
and I was seeing, the whole flight back to Cu Chi,
a girl turning her elegant face away
after I'd said all I had to say.
This was in Viet Nam. Who didn't love me.

ALLSTON JAMES

Honor (1969)

I'm not sure at what point
He finally died but it was
Clear that he would never survive.
After the chopper lifted him out
Of the jungle there was nothing
Left to do but sit with a kid I
Barely knew, both of us crying
In the rain and trying to light
Each other's cigarettes, the blood
Still warm and alive upon our palms.

YUSEF KOMUNYAKAA

Somewhere Near Phu Bai

The moon cuts through
night trees like a circular saw
white hot. In the guardshack
I lean on the sandbags,
taking aim at whatever.
Hundreds of bluesteel stars
cut a path, fanning out
silver for a second. If anyone's
there, don't blame me.

I count the shapes ten meters
out front, over & over, making sure
they're always there.
I don't dare blink an eye.
The white-painted backs
of the Claymore mines
like quarter moons.
They say Victor Charlie will
paint the other sides & turn
the blast toward you.

If I hear a noise
will I push the button
& blow myself away?
The moon grazes treetops.
I count the Claymores again.
Thinking about buckshot

kneaded in the plastic C-4
of the brain, counting
sheep before I know it.

Starlight Scope Myopia

Gray-blue shadows lift
shadows onto an ox cart.

Making night work for us,
the starlight scope brings
men into killing range.

The river under Vi Bridge
takes the heart away

like the Water God
riding his dragon.
Smoke-colored

Viet Cong
move under our eyelids,

lords over loneliness
winding like coralvine through
sandalwood & lotus,

inside our skulls years
after this scene ends.

The brain closes down
to get the job done. What
looks like one step into the trees,

they're lifting crates of ammo

& sacks of rice, swaying

under their shared weight.
Caught in the infrared,
what are they saying?

Are they talking about women
or calling the Americans

beaucoup dien cai dau?
One of them is laughing.
You want to place a finger

to his lips & say "shhhh."
You try reading ghost-talk

on their lips. They say
"up-up we go," lifting as one.
This one, old, bowlegged,

you feel you could reach out
& take him into your arms. You

peer down the sights of your M-16,
seeing the full moon
loaded on an ox cart.

A Break from the Bush

The South China Sea drives in
its herd of wild blue horses.
We go at the volleyball like a punchingbag:
Clem's already lost a tooth
& Johnny's got a kisser

closing his left eye.
Frozen airlifted steaks burn
on a wire grill, & miles away
we hear machineguns go crazy.
Pretending we're somewhere else,
we play harder.
Lee Otis, the point man,
high on Buddha grass,
buries himself up to his neck
in sand, saying, "Can you see me now?
This is the spot where they're gonna
build a Hilton. Invest in Paradise.
Bang bozos! You're dead."
Frenchie's cassette player
unravels Hendrix's "Purple Haze."
Snake, 17, from Daytona,
sits at the water's edge,
the ash on his cigarette
points like a crooked gray
finger to the ground. CJ,
who in three days will trip
a fragmentation mine,
runs after the ball
into the whitecaps,
laughing.

Tiger Lady

Dressed as a drag queen
with a .45, he glides along
air, on magic, on his Honda
shooting American officers.
Viet Cong Tiger Lady
hidden by Saigon nights, eyes

like stones on a riverbottom.
In his breezy ao dai
he's a cheap thrill,
gunning his motorcycle,
headed for a tunnel
in the back of his mind
lit by nothing but blood,
just a taillight
outdistancing the echo
of bluesteel & heartbeat.

The Dead at Quang Tri

Captain Gungho, my men
are getting real jumpy.
Those we kill get up from
our ambushes & walk away.
We search trees. Like bygones,
if only they'd be done with,
the body counts would mean
something. But this is
harder than counting shadows
of shadows & stones along paths
going nowhere, the way a tiger
circles & backtracks by
smelling its blood on the ground.
The one kneeling beside the pagoda,
remember him? Captain, we won't
talk about that. The Buddhist boy
at the gate with the shaven head
we rubbed for luck
glides by like a white moon.
He won't stay dead, dammit!
Blades aim for the family jewels,

the grass we walk on
won't stay down.

After the Fall of Saigon

An afternoon storm has hit
the Pearl of the Orient
& stripped nearly everybody.
Bandoliers, miniskirts, tennis shoes,
fatigue jackets, combat boots—
the city's color bruised, polyester
suits limping down sidestreets.
Even the ragpicker is glad
to let his Australian bush hat
with the red feather float away.

Something deeper than sadness
litters the alleys.
The old mama-san who always
collected scraps of yellow paper,
cigarette butts & matchsticks
through field-stripped years
hides under her cardboard box.
Cowboys park new Harleys
along Lam Son Square
& do their disappearing act.

Dzung leaves the Continental Hotel
in a newspaper dress,
hoping for a hard rain.
Moving through broken colors
flung to the ground,
she sings, tries not to,
mixing up the words to Trinh's

"Mad Girl's Love Song"
& "Stars Fell on Alabama,"
trying to bite off her tongue.

Boat People

After midnight they load up.
A hundred shadows move about blindly.
Something close to sleep
hides low voices drifting
toward a red horizon. Tonight's
a blue string, the moon's pull—
this boat's headed somewhere.
Lucky to have gotten past
searchlights low-crawling the sea,
like a woman shaking water
from her long dark hair.

Calm over everything, a change
of heart. Twelve times in three days
they've been lucky,
clinging to each other in gray mist.
Now Thai fishermen gaze out across
the sea as it changes color,
hands shading their eyes
like sailors do,
minds on robbery & rape.
Sunlight burns blood-orange
till nothing makes sense.
Storm warnings crackle from a radio.
Gold shines in their teeth.
The Thai fishermen turn away.
Not enough water for the trip.
The boat people cling to each other,

their faces like yellow sea grapes,
wounded by doubt & salt air.
Dusk hangs over the water.
Sea sick, they daydream Jade Mountain
a whole world away, half-drunk
on what they hunger to become.

HERBERT KROHN

Can Tho

Can Tho, *favela* of crowing cocks
    favela of my dreams
Can Tho's tin rooftops conduct the rains
    to Can Tho's muddy streams
Her swallows turn and veer in the sun
    and sing in whistles and screams

I love the gentle people of this city—
fragile as birdsong, flexible as rice
yet birds can awaken armies
and rice can sing in the wind.
I love this race of farmers and musicians
with a love that no more needs returning
than a love for bread and songs.

American soldiers,
the cocks of Can Tho crowed when you arrived here
like Can Tho's women cooing
"no sweat, I love you too much"
when first you meet.
American soldiers,
the cocks that crow at morning and at evening
will crow triumphantly at your departure
like Can Tho's women nursing
fatherless children whom you never knew.

Farmer's Song at Can Tho

What is a man but a farmer,
bowels and a heart that sings,
who plants his rice in season
bowing then to the river.
I am a farmer and I know what I know.
This month's harvest is tall green rice.
Next month's harvest is hordes of hungry beetles.
How can peace come to a green country?

Ferryman's Song at Binh Minh

Vendors of green oranges . vendors of immaculate
 ducks
Children, lame musicians . begging with milky eyes
Ancients with their boys . they are moving altogether
Riding the back of the dragon . crossing the *Rach Can
Tho*

My Flute

When I had learned enough to fail every test
I began to play a flute called "blueman's rainbow"
color of the third rail
engines keep kissing
to make them strong and travel.
My flute called "enemy of silence"
frees every prisoner
in the midnight special hour

when silver chimes with the silver
moon quarter
of a million miles away.
Nothing inside my flute then
measures the nothing that keeps us apart.
My flute called "what is your real name?"
says no to loaded questions.
Three joints it has like a finger
point to an open door
but me and my flute called "second nature now"
stay in the empty window the world goes by.

LUCY LAKIDES

Armed Forces

At midnight, I wake to a breeze
over my ribs like cool hands.
Moonlight and streetlight
fall on the black
and silent telephone.
I wait for the airline
to announce your arrival,
for postcards
from Washington galleries
saying, "eggs Florentine,
Miro, 'our nation's capital.' "
Instead, I hear of civil
service, a rise
to power, the Pentagon.
My curtains move a little.
In the sky, tiny red and white
blinking lights could be bombers.

Your mother asks me to tea,
your father calls from time to time,
both to be certain I'm still
waiting as women should wait
for men in uniform, men
hidden in photographs, men
who write about stockings,
jazz and armoured cars, men
who return in jets every six months
to continue what should never continue

but never ends: a weird airstream.
But I could be the soldier
and you could wait for me instead
while I, in my parachute, fall
suddenly into a stranger's garden:

> He stands to the side, perplexed:
> I'm the largest bird he's ever seen.
> Then he takes me inside,
> feeds me brandied pears,
> touches my breasts, asks
> of my home in the West.
> The patio doors are open.
> We see moonlight
> and starlight, feel light
> wind on our faces.
> He's been expecting me.

After this night,
I know
I can kill anyone.
You pace in a darkened hotel room
thinking of my anger, my voice,
my hair, while outside your window
birds are settling arguments.
You imagine me in dark green silk
with pilot's wings on my collar.
You dial the phone
but I've pulled out the wires.
You send flowers
but neighbors steal them.
Your letters get lost
and end up in London.

But remember I asked you to stay,
to walk along the lake at dawn,

to share a bunker, some C-rations.
What could be better in wartime?
The plane that brought me over
took you away.

JAMES LAUGHLIN

The Kind-

hearted Americans are
adopting Vietnamese

orphans it makes them
feel better about what

happened they did not
want what happened to

happen & did not think
things like that would

happen because so many
wise men told them they

couldn't if you had e-
nough liberty & napalm

and honor and airbombs
it's really sad about

the Americans the way
they're so kindhearted.

MCAVOY LAYNE

On the Yellow Footprints

"Well now, look at this unsightly herd,
Standin' there passin' the crud to one another
Without even movin'.
My name is Briant, girls.
I'm your mother now,
And I'm going to give you some motherly advice,
Quit on me,
And I'll show you a short cut back to the old
Neighborhood,
Right through your ass.
Is that clear!?"

"Yes, Sir!"

"I don't hear you, ladies!"

"Yes, Sir!!"

"Puberty must be hell."

"Yes, Sir!!!"

The Mob

"You, mob,
Are about to be transformed

Into a fighting unit.
You will be taught to immobilize
Maim
Or
Kill a man
With your bare hands
In six seconds.
But don't get any funny ideas, girls,
We
Got
It
Down
To
Four.''

Gettin' Straight

It was a warm September night
When Third Marines approached the coast.
There were flashings of light
And memories
Of faraway Camp Pendleton
When Wrong-Way McCauly gazed out to sea
And asked,

"Is that the same ocean that takes us to Vietnam?"

And someone said,

"Wrong-Way, this time you're right."

And
He
Grinned.

Guns

When the M-16 rifle had a stoppage,
One could feel enemy eyes
Climbing
His
Bones
Like
Ivy.

On Hats & Things

Gunny Harlabakis
Was a lifer.
He'd hold a weapons inspection
In the eye of a hurricane.
No one had told Gunny Harlabakis
That this was one place in the Marine Corps
Where you don't play fahck-fahck
With the troopies.
$120
In
A
Hat
Got
Him
Killed.

Beautiful Ladies

Women
Have
A
Way
Of
Making
Heroes
Out
Of
The
Poor
Bozos
Who
Go
Off
To
Do
The
Killing.

Intersection in the Sky

The Air Force called it Quadrant Bombing.
The pilot simply flew north from Da Nang
Along a radar beam
To the intersection of another beam
Originating from a carrier
In the South China Sea.
At the intersection it happened.
Automatic.

Right on the old grid square,
The first payload collapsing three bunkers
At the rock pile
Killing one marine.
That
Was
When
Bombs
Were
Dumb.

Collect Call

"Good afternoon, General Ball,
Are we able to speak with Corporal Murphy?
Corporal Murphy, this is the President speaking
From Washington, on behalf of all America, in
Commending you on your personal courage
In these troubled times.
Your parents, Mr. & Mrs. Murphy,
Are here in Washington to accept
The Silver Star for gallantry awarded you
By the Marine Corps.
And I want to assure you, Corporal Murphy,
Along with the rest of our boys over there,
That we are working to bring you home
To enjoy once again
What you have fought so hard to preserve."

"Thank you, Mr. President. It's encouraging
To all of us here to hear those words,
Encouraging even to the North Vietnamese.
I'm convinced they'd like to get rid of us."

DENISE LEVERTOV

Excerpt from "Staying Alive"

May 14th, 1969—Berkeley
Went with some of my students to work in the People's
Park. There seemed to be plenty of digging and
  gardening
help so we decided, as Jeff had his truck available, to
  shovel
up the garbage that had been thrown into the west part
  of
the lot and take it out to the city dump.
              O happiness
              in the sun! Is it
              that simple, then,
              to live?
              —crazy rhythm of
              scooping up barehanded
              (all the shovels already in use)
              careless of filth and broken glass
              —scooping up garbage together
              poets and dreamers studying
              joy together, clearing
              refuse off the neglected, newly
                  recognized,
humbly waiting ground, place, locus, of what could be
  our
New World even now, our revolution, one and one and
one and one together, black children swinging, green
guitars, that energy, that music, no one
              telling anyone what to do,

169

everyone doing,
each leaf of
the new grass near us
a new testament . . .
Out to the dump:
acres of garbage glitter and stink in wild sunlight, gulls
float and scream in the brilliant sky,
polluted waters bob and dazzle, we laugh, our arms
  ache,
                              we work together
shoving and kicking and scraping to empty our
  truckload
                                    over the bank
even though we know
the irony of adding to the Bay fill, the System has us
  there—

but we love each other and return to the Park

Thursday, May 15th
At 6 a.m. the ominous zooming, war-sound, of
  helicopters
breaks into our sleep.

To the Park:
ringed with police,
Bulldozers have moved in.
Barely awake, the people—
those who had made for each other
a green place—
begin to gather at the corners.

Their tears fall on sidewalk cement.
The fence goes up, twice a man's height
Everyone knows (yet no one yet
believes it) what all shall know
this day, and the days that follow:

now, the clubs, the gas,
bayonets, bullets. The War

comes home to us . . .

LOU LIPSITZ

The Feeding

We sit in the darkness
and the baby drinks from you.
Alive! I cannot
believe it.

We are silent.
Far off, great explosives
stand in hundreds of holes
sucked out of the planet;
millions of men
who might have befriended each other
prowl the earth's surface
as hunters.

You open your eyes
and look at me
and I see you are satisfied.
The baby sleeps.
You have nourished what you can,
which is no small triumph
in a starved time.

DICK LOURIE

For All My Brothers and Sisters

this is not easy to write about   it involves
the ignorant peasants shot by the A-
merican soldiers   these peasants were so
ignorant they had no names   so primitive
in nature they were all indistinguishable
from one another   so like dumb animals
their language was babbling nonsense   and when
they died all you could remember was their
gestures   clinging together in the ditch

PAUL MARTIN

Watching the News

From out there, the news keeps coming
focusing here in front of the couch:
    mountains of shoes and eyeglasses;
    the limousine turning the corner, forward,
    backward, slowed down, enlarged, and stopped;
    that naked girl running toward me,
    her back aflame with napalm—
these pictures that make it difficult to mow the lawn
to replace a burned out bulb or the brick

above the door where the starling returns each year
to build her nest. For weeks I watched her carry
each strand and now the eggs have hatched
on a narrow ledge inside the wall.
Though I can't see their blind eyes, their stretching
    necks
I can hear them as soon as she enters the hole.
                    Last year
trying their wings toward the light, they tipped
the nest deeper into the wall.
At night I could hear their faint chirping
from somewhere near the bottom.
I promised then I'd repair that hole,
but here it is another Spring
and the starling continues to fly out and in
dropping food into the silence
and I can feel my chances piling up
like small, delicate bones in the darkness.

GERALD MCCARTHY

Excerpts from "War Story"

1   Med Building
They brought the dead
in helicopters and trucks
and tried to piece the bodies back together,
shoved them in plastic bags
to be sent home.
Sometimes there was an arm or leg
leftover,
it lay around until the next shipment;
they made it fit in somewhere.

7
Flares in a night sky
lighting up the place
like a football field.
Ammo belts
strung over shoulders,
I remember the time
I was a newsboy
with the sunday morning papers,
throwing the headlines.

8
We found him
his chest torn open,
shirt sticky brown.
A corporal with a bayonet
cut off his ears,

and kicked the body
in passing.

9

They shot the woman in the arm,
four of them
raped her
and killed an old man
who tried to interfere;
and later killed the woman too.
She was the enemy.

11

Hot sun,
I walk into a whorehouse
pay the girl
unbuckle my pants
and screw her
sweat sticking to my fatigues
small legs grasping my back
her slanted eyes look up at me
as I come.
Outside the tin-roofed hut
another GI waits his turn.

12

That night in the bunker,
we shared some smoke
and stared out at the stars.
Then,
the mortars blasted
choking sulfur
shoving the magazines in
round after round
deaf,
blinded,
hugging the dirt,
I pissed my pants.

Later,
confusion gone,
you all shot to shit,
you black bastard.
Fuck.

14

In the early morning the working party
came and filled in the remains of the bunker
with sand. The bodies had been removed
the night before, but the stench lingered.
Soon the earth was worn down smooth by
the boots of the soldiers. They moved off
to build another bunker along the line.

Clinging to a bush was a dirty piece of
utility jacket. A breeze was blowing in off
the ocean. It rattled the pop cans on the
concertina wire and made hollow, tinny
noises.

17

Well, I said, I came back.
Grandpa pulled the hat down over his eyes
smiled at me in his sleep.
They asked if I wanted breakfast,
some coffee maybe?
Had it been a long ride?
My father looked older.
I smoked a cigarette,
watched the shadows leave the backyard
back into the old house,
my stepmother's chatter,
the old man's sadness
so early in the morning.

19

John Bradt said, It'll be all right
when he gets home.

* * *

The farmers in Hale valley are waiting
for the sun to rise.
The train winds slowly
through the mountains.
A voice of strangers
knocking politely
on doors.
The soldiers are coming home,
they carry the sadness with them
like others carry groceries
or clothes in from the line.
There is no music in the parade;
the sound of their coming
waits at the bottoms of rivers,
stones rubbing against each other
in the current.

Arrival

There it is again
the roll of cars in wet streets
hours crushed together in the rain.

I come back to the voices
to their eyes
to a hand turning up a collar in the crowds
to a dark street in the snow.

I lower myself back
my feet in doorways
silence like a rope behind me.

Yes, this must be the right street
and they must be my friends
the stares buttoned to their lapels.
I follow them all the way.

* * *

This is where I wanted to get off
in a new winter
on this avenue of trees
the sound of wings
and the wind
wrapping itself around me.

The same glow in windows
and my hands on the hours
on the empty glasses.
The days stuffed in my pocket
like old addresses
and my coat too thin
for this cold.

Finding the Way Back

Morning.
Two sparrows sit on the tin roof
puffing themselves up
like old men in a park.
The longest war of this century
refuses to be ended.
I watch them signing their peace
with twelve different pens
live on t.v.

I remember the ocean
the breeze off the water
sunlight through the curtains of rain.
The young men running
darkness falling around their shoulders.
The children gone
their hearts in open throats.

The faces
the last columns of smoke
tearing the pages from my eyes.

There was never anything to come back to.
Aubrey knew it at Binh San
under the afternoon sun
staring into death.
My brother
I went on living.
There was nothing else
I could do.

The Sound of Guns

1
The sparrow hawk drops to the cornfield
and in the same motion rises.
December's cold tightens around me,
a spider's web frozen white against the glass.

All day the sky is bleak with the coming snow,
the hours seem to pause like the bird
caught in an uplift of wind.
Out back the hay lies in rolls
the cows huddled together near the water troughs.

The highway runs past the brown fields
all the way west to Omaha, and just keeps going.
At the university in town
tight-lipped men tell me the war in Vietnam is over,
that my poems should deal with other things:
earth, fire, water, air.

2
A friend told me once

that ours was a generation of love;
and I know he meant that this was a generation
that took too much, that turned from one death
to another.

I don't know what it is that's kept me going.
At nineteen I stood at night and watched
an airfield mortared. A plane that was to take
me home, burning; men running out of the flames.

Seven winters have slipped away,
the war still follows me.
Never in anything have I found
a way to throw off the dead.

The Fall of Da Nang

Tonight the newspapers report
the air-lift evacuation of Da Nang has failed;
that South Vietnamese soldiers shot their way
through crowds of civilians
to board the last plane that landed.

Years have passed since Aubrey and I
got high together, watching the night sky
across the South China Sea.
Near Monkey Mountain the Viet-Cong are entrenched
hitting the airfield with artillery fire.

I think back to an evening in July
in that same city, when I waited for a plane
to get me out.
My friends watch television.

* * *

I pry open the window, listen to the noise
of a passing car on the wet road.
The news interrupts a commercial
with a special bulletin. I watch the faces
of Vietnamese children: the same tired faces
that will always be there.

My friends leave to play poker:
nickel, dime, quarter, they say.
I smoke cigarettes, drink beer.
It's Saturday night, the end of March.

The Hooded Legion

Let us put up a monument to the lie.
JOSEPH BRODSKY

There are no words here
to witness why we fought,
who sent us or what we hoped to gain.

There is only the rain
as it streaks the black stone,
these memories of rain
that come back to us—
a hooded legion reflected in a wall.

Tonight we wander weaponless and cold
along this shore of the Potomac
like other soldiers who camped here
looking out over smoldering fires into the night.

* * *

What did we dream of
the summer before we went away?
What leaf did not go silver
in the last light?
What hand did not turn us aside?

WALTER MCDONALD

The Winter Before the War

In fall we raked
the leaves downhill
in heaps high
as the fence,
set them afire
and watched them
burn. In hours
the fire died down,
the mounds of leaves
only a smudge
of black.

Weeks later
the first snow fell.
Weeks after that
the lake one hundred
yards away was solid,
white, the ice so thick
trucks drove on it.
Fishermen wrapped up like bears
chopped through the ice,
let down their hooks
and waited. Their breaths
resembled chimney smoke.
We pulled the sled
across the lake,
our children
bundled up

and eating snow.
The fireplace
after dark
was where we thawed.
Chocolate steamed
in mugs we wrapped
our hands around.
Our children slept.
The news came on.
We watched
each other's eyes.

For Kelly,
Missing in Action

When you disappeared
over the North
I pulled down *Dubliners*.

What strange counterparts,
you and the Cong.
You, who said no one would make
General
reading Joyce,
named your F-4 "The Dead,"
and dropped out of the sun
like some death angel
playing mumbledy peg
with bombs.

I never knew what launched
the search for Araby in you,
that wholly secular search
for thrills.

* * *

I wonder how you felt
when they strapped on the bombs
that first flight North.
Did it seem at all like
bearing a chalice through a throng of
foes, or finally,
as you let them go
did you see yourself in the plexiglass
a creature masked
derided by vanity
dead as Dublin,
far from home?

Faraway Places

This daughter watching ducks knows
nothing of Vietnam,
this pond her only Pacific,
separation to her
only the gulf between herself
and ducks that others feed.
"They will come," he calms her, "soon,"
and touches her. Her hair blows
golden in the wind. Strange prospect
to leave such gold, he thinks.
There is no gold for him
in Asia.

The ducks parade unsatisfied,
now gliding to her hand, her bread,
her tenderness. Possession
turns on him like swimming ducks,
forcing his touch again.

* * *

She does not feel his claim
upon her gold
that swirls upon her face but cannot blink
her eyes
so full of ducks.

War Games

Crouched in a sandbagged bunker,
lights out, listening for rockets,
we played the game with nothing
in our hands, pretending dice

clicked in our fists and hit the dirt floor
rolling. Snake eyes, boxcars,
the point to make, someone
calling our luck, no one

we could see, all of us in this
together. Rockets that crashed down
on the base always killed somebody else.
We played with nothing to lose,

the crews on night shift
risking no more than us,
no sand bunker safe from a hit.
We rolled till our luck ran out,

passed the empty handful
to the next man kneeling
in the dark, bunkered down,
having the time of our lives.

* * *

We never knew the color of scrip
we lost, not caring
what was at stake in night games,
not daring to think.

When the all-clear siren wailed
we lifted our winnings from dust
and left through the reeking tunnel
into moonlight naked as day

and climbed the steps of our barracks
to wire springs tight as our nerves,
lying in rooms flashing red
from flames in the distance.

Caliban in Blue

Off again,
thrusting up at scald
of copper in orient west
I climb into such blue skies.
Skies even here
belong to Setobos:
calls it air power.
Air power is peace power,
his motto catechizes
as we, diving, spout
flame from under,
off in one hell
of a roar.

His arms like radar
point the spot.
For this, I trained to salivate
and tingle, target-diving,

hand enfolding hard throttle
in solitary masculine delight.

Focused on cross hairs,
eyes glazing, hand triggers switches in
pulsing orgasm,
savage release;
pull out
and off we go again
thrusting deep
into the martial lascivious blue
of uncle's sky.

Interview
with a Guy Named Fawkes,
U.S. Army

——you tell them this——
tell them shove it, they're
not here, tell them kiss
my rear when they piss about
women and kids in shacks
we fire on. damn.
they fire on us.
hell yes, it's war
they sent us for.
what do they know back where
not even in their granddam's days
did any damn red rockets glare.
don't tell me
how chips fall.
those are The Enemy:
waste them all.

Rocket Attack

(AP)—Enemy gunners lobbed seven Russian-made
100 lb. rockets into the American base at Cam Ranh
Bay last night. Damage was reported light. Four
Americans were wounded, and three Vietnamese civil-
ians were killed.

Rocks fallout on us
like mountains,
crash of those impacting
richer than thunder,
concussion sharp as wood on wood
slamming shut my coffin.

Another on its way
maybe

seconds

like lightning
within
bursting,
smashing everything.

Little mouths
little hands I saw
in the Vietnamese airmen's
shacks—
little laughter
clipped, shrill, grating
on my western nerves.
Daughter, oh God, my daughter
may she never
safe at home

Never hear the horrible
sucking sound a rocket makes when it

For Harper,
Killed in Action

When they brought you down
over the Plain of Jars
I thought of when you
volunteered for photo runs
from Udorn into Laos.
Better to take pictures
than to bomb, you said.
I do not blame. My taxes
paid your fares.

I hope it was a lucky shot,
sudden,
not some gunner blinded to your loss
cheering as your solid
flesh impacted
in the common ground.

Veteran

I get as far as the park
this time.
Spectators queer as animals
circle me like a campfire.
They hope I'll fall.

Leaves lie in the park
like tiny bombs

ready to explode. Someday
someone raking
will strike a fuse.
We'll all be killed.

My stumps itch
inside their legs,
lightweight aluminum
clump clump. One of my arms
goes out of control, shifts smoothly
like a transmission, salutes.

They think I'm
shooting a bone
at them. I'm trying
to turn back. They're closing in,
this is Da Nang, their eyes
rake me like AK-47s.

The Retired Pilot
to Himself

I come to the simplest things
last. Even flying
I was slow,
rehearsing take-offs before sleep,
spinning solo
others merely logged as spun.
Last discovering the fun
meant war—
chandelles and Immelmanns
and Cuban Eights,
ecstatic murder in the skies too strange,
too wonderful to grasp.

* * *

Bombs so long falling; after falling,
what release?
                    O for tonight—
my child
with benediction
sidling heel and toe in graceful
rhapsody,
acceptance of herself.

Once You've Been to War

There are times when everything I touch
turns to leaves, my plot of earth breathing
like women who seem to be always fertile,
their nurseries teeming with mouths,
flower-print dresses forever bulging.

Whatever I plant at night in dreams
by dawn has rooted, ferns like veils,
orchids, fuchsia tendrils reaching for trees,
my secret back yard dense as the front,
three canopies of rain forest

chittering with spider monkeys,
toucans, orange and black minahs,
birds of paradise. And there are times
deep in my pillow below three canopies
of rain forest I did not plant

but helped to burn, the sandbags burst
and sand blows over everything.
Concertina wire can't hold it back.
Roaches blue-bronzed and emerald,
the size of condors,

* * *

tweezer their way over dunes
the winds shuffle and fold like cards.
Rockets slam down beyond the trees,
fallout clatters the leaves
like hail. In parched riverbeds

fish keep flopping,
jets diving are lightning without rain,
and in the distance, bombs explode so long
the hollows of my knees flutter
like flutes whittled from bone.

Hauling Over Wolf Creek Pass
in Winter

If I make it over the pass
I park the rig, crawl back to the bunk
and try to sleep, the pigs swaying
like a steep grade, like the last curve
Johnson took too fast and burned.
But that was summer. His fire
spread to the next county.

It doesn't worry me.
I take the east climb no sweat
and the rest is a long coasting
down to the pens in Pagosa Springs.
It's the wolves I wait for.
We never see them any other way,
not in this business.
Sometimes five, six hauls before
propped on one arm, smoking,
I see them slink from the dark pines
toward the truck. They drive the pigs
crazy, squealing

as if a legion of demons had them.
Later, when I start up and go,
the pigs keep plunging,
trying to drive us over the cliff.

I let them squeal, their pig hearts
exploding like grenades.
The wolves are dark and silent.
Kneeling, I watch them split up
like sappers, some in the tree lines,
some gliding from shadow to shadow,
red eyes flashing in moonlight,
some farther off, guarding the flanks.
Each time, they know they have me.

I take my time, knowing I can crawl
over the seat, light up,
sip from the steaming thermos.
I crank the diesel,
release the air brakes
like a rocket launcher.
Wolves run in circles. I hit the lights.
Wolves plunge through deep snow
to the trees, the whole pack starving.
Revving up, the truck rolls down the highway
faster, the last flight out of Da Nang.
I shove into third gear, fourth,
the herd of pigs screaming, the load
lurching and banging on every turn,
almost delivered, almost airborne.

THOMAS MCGRATH

Reading the Names of the Vietnam War Dead

For a long day and a night we read the names:
Many thousand brothers fallen in the green and distant
    land . . .

Sun going south after the autumn equinox.
By night the vast moon: "Moon of the Falling
    Leaves";
Our voices hoarse in the cold of the first October rains.
And the long winds of the season to carry our words
    away.

The citizens go on about their business.
By night sleepers condense in the houses grown cloudy
    with dreams.
By day a few come to hear us and leave, shaking their
    heads
Or cursing. On Sunday the moral animal prays in his
    church.

It is Fall; but a host of dark birds flies toward the cold
    North.
Thousands of dense black stones fall forever through
    the darkness under the earth.

Go Ask the Dead

1

The soldier, past full retreat, is marching out of the
    grave
As he lies under dying grass in the slow judgment of
    time
On which he has lost his grasp.
                              And lost his taste as
                                    well—
For, tell-tale as fast as it will, no tongue can put salt on
    his name.
The captain sun has done with this numberless
    underground.

2

He has seeded out of that flesh where the flashing
    lights first fade
In the furry sky of the head.
                              And the orient admiral
                                    brain
Has seen its images go like ensigns blown from a
    line—
Those raving signals.
                    All quality's bled from his light,
And number (he's all thumbs now) divides where
    infinities fail.

3

Grand winds of the sky might claim; or the blue hold
Of ocean accept;
                    or fire sublime—
                              though it's earth
Now hinders and halters
                    him.

But those underground
birds, his bones,
(Homeless all havens save here) fly out of their low-
hilled heavens
And shine up into the light to blaze in his land's long
lie.

4
And long they lie there but not for love in the windy
contentions
Of sun and rain, shining. This endless invasion of
death
Darkens our world. There is no argument that will
move them.
"You are eating our light!" they cry. "Where have
you taken the sun?
You have climbed to the moon on a ladder of dead
man's bones!"

RICHARD M. MISHLER

Ceremony

The 'copter lays flat the rice stalks
as it first hovers and then rises over the water
with the pilot pulling back on the stick.
The abducted, a fulvous skinned farmer, watches
his hamlet shrink into a tear.

Another Vietnamese aboard, hands bound
behind his back, with the rope looped tight
around his neck, stares with suspicion.

Both wear black, worn shiny, silk pajamas.
The bound one has no shirt over his scarred,
emaciated chest, while the farmer wears a buttonless
US Army jungle shirt, with one sergeant stripe hanging
on the left sleeve. It is permanently sweat-stained.

The 'copter flies lazily 2,000 feet above the paddies.
Through an interpreter, the American Lt.
asks the farmer three quick questions.
He replies with the same quickness. He doesn't know.
He is only a farmer, a poor man with half a crop
and half a family. A poor farmer who knows nothing,
nothing. Two more questions are asked of him,
    knowing
he is only a farmer and cannot know. And nothing.
One more, with the threat of him being dropped
from the 'copter. Tears of fear and resignation fall.

* * *

Without ceremony, he is shoved over the side.
He seems to glide. His scream floats up to the ears
of the bound VC, whose muscles tighten against the
    ropes.
The water buffalo jumps at the splash, and the
sucking mud swallows the crumpled body, buries him
in the ground of his ancestors. The sun burns
in the sky - incensed.

Even before the questions are asked of the VC,
the Lt. knows he will talk. And the VC knows he
will not, because he knows the sun also burns for
him; his ancestors are also below. Already
the cricket's chirp fills his marrow.

LARRY MOFFI

Putting an End to the War Stories

Dust storms whipped
around us
as if summer had baked
the earth to clay,
tumbleweeds
buttressed the underpass
of the interstate,
and we drove on drunk
as ever, knocking them
over an invisible horizon
like huge spores
or tiny parachutes
collapsing
acres away
in a shorn field
where a farmer
threw his rake at the sky.

That is how
I convinced myself
I would remember it,
but the weather
in truth
was simply unseasonable,
the war over.
It was May,
and I sat home
watching dandelions

pop in the thick
of the new lawn
when you arrived
weary from the blind
drive across Kansas
and those winds.

In other words,
we who were once soldiers,
the best of buddies
with stories of rank,
detail, and order to tell
in our own small company,
had less than sadness
left to speak of.
So we talked at great length
of divisions, inventing
the unusual in weather
and circumstance,
while the eaves
covered us
and rain slapped
the porch
and the grass grew.

JAMES MOORE

One Reason I Went to Prison

A boat gathers you in,
fools you by rocking gently,
makes you feel you're safe
as the waves gently lap
at the prow. When it
goes down, women and children
escape first, the men
work together as heroes.
Then, the time comes,
it's you and your father,
sink or swim, neither
can swim without the other,
each sinks separately
going his own direction
down and down and down.
Yet something solid finally
grabs your ankles, sand
under you, push up, the surface
is not so far away, your
father is not dead either
even says
"He must be brave."
It was the only chance
I had to show you I could
make it alone, over my head.
If I had known we'd go together,

even to the bottom of my own grief,
maybe, then, it would have been
unnecessary to prove myself
your enemy.

DAVID MURA

The Natives

Several months after we lost our way,
they began to appear, their quiet eyes
assuring us, their small painted legs
scurrying beside us. By then our radio
had been gutted by fungus, our captain's cheek
stunned by a single bullet; our ammo vanished
the first night we discovered our maps were useless,
our compasses a lie. The second week
forced us on snakes, monkeys, lizards, and toads;
we ate them raw over wet smoking fires.
Waking one morning we found a riverboat
loaded with bodies hanging in the trees
like an ox on a sling, marking the stages
of flood. One of us thought he heard the whirr
of a chopper, but it was only the monsoon
drumming the leaves, soaking our skin so damp
you felt you could peel it back to scratch
the bones of your ankle. Gradually our names
fell from our mouths, never heard again.
Nights, faces glowing, we told stories of wolves,
and the jungle seemed colder, more a home.

And then we glimpsed them, like ghosts of children
darting through the trees, the curtain of rain;
we told each other nothing, hoping they'd vanish.
But one evening the leaves parted. Slowly
they emerged and took our hands, their striped
faces dripping, looking up in wonder

at our grizzled cheeks. Stumbling like gods
without powers, we carried on our backs
what they could not carry, the rusted grenades,
the ammoless rifles, barrels clotted with flies.
They waited years before they brought us
to their village, led us in circles till
time disappeared. Now, stone still, our feet
tangled with vines, we stand by their doorways
like soft-eyed virgins in the drilling rain:
the hair on our shoulders dangles and shines.

Huy Nguyen: Brothers, Drowning Cries

1

Shaking the snow from your hair, bowl cut
like an immigrant's, you hand me your assignment—
Compare and Contrast. Though your accent stumbles
like my grandfather's, you talk of Faulkner,
The Sound and the Fury. You mention Bergson,
whom you've read in French. *Duree.* How the moment
    lasts.
Your paper opens swimming the Mekong Delta.

2

As you lift your face, the sun flashes
down wrinkles of water; blue dragonflies
dart overhead. You hear your brother call.
You go under again, down, down, till you
reach the bottom, a fistful of river clay,
mold a ball in the dark, feel your lungs struggle,
waiting to burst—

        Where is your brother?

Against the current's thick drag, stumble

to shore, the huts of fishermen—
My brother, my brother's drowned!

Faces emerge from dark doorways,
puzzled, trotting towards you, then
all of them running to the river,
diving and searching the bottom
not for clay but flesh,

and there the man

crawls up on the beach, your brother
slumped over his shoulder, bouncing up
and down as the man runs up and down,
water belching from your brother's mouth
but no air, not air; flings
your brother to the ground, bends,
puts mouth to your brother's lips,
blows in, blows out, until your brother's
chest expands once, once, and once,
and his eyes flutter open, not yet back
in this world, not yet recognizing the blue
of the sky, that your people see as happiness,
even happier than the sun.

3

It's five years since you sailed the South China Sea
and the night Thai pirates sliced your wife's finger for
a ring, then beat you senseless. You woke to a
    merchant ship
passing in silence, as if a mirage were shouting for
    help.
Later, in that camp in Manila, loudspeakers told the
    story
of a boat broken on an island reef, and the survivors
thrashing through the waves, giving up the ghost,
and the girl who reached the shore and watched
the others, one by one, fall from starvation,

as she drank after each rain from shells on the beach.
At last only her brother remained, his eyes staring
upwards at the wind and sun, calling, calling her
    name. . . .
The camp went silent, then a baby, a woman sobbing
And you knew someone was saved to tell the story.

4

Huy,
how many ships are drifting just out of the harbor of
    history,
all waiting for a voice, like a tug boat, to pull the
    survivors
into port? (Each of them sings a skeletal song—*Who
    shall be saved?*)
At seventy, through the streets of Saigon, your mother
    hauls
bowls of soup to sell at dawn. In prison, malaria numbs
    your
brother's limbs. You wait for his death. Safe. Fat. A
    world away.
You are a man without a country, a citizen of this
    century,
and if I ask you to write this down, you do so with a
    smile
of sorrow and amusement. And where you swim each
    night, what wakes you
screaming, remains beyond your English or my
    ignorance.

PERRY OLDHAM

War Stories

Have you heard Howard's tape?
You won't believe it:
He recorded the last mortar attack.
The folks at home have never heard a real
Mortar attack
And he wants to let them know
Exactly
What it's like.

Every night he pops popcorn
And drinks Dr. Pepper
And narrates the tape:
  Ka-blooie!
  Thirty-seven rounds of eighty millimeter—
  You can count them if you slow down the tape.
  There's an AK.
  Those are hand grenades.
  Here's where the Cobras come in
  And whomp their ass.

Noon

I'm digging holes for three wilted saplings—
pin oak, mulberry, flowering crab—
behind a tract house reeking freshly sawn
boards in the heat of a July afternoon.

CARRYING THE DARKNESS

After 22 years in dorm rooms, the Air Force,
a string of roach-filled apartments and rent
houses, I am a home owner. Transparencies
swarming from my hat, I squat on my heels
among clods of red clay and green shoots of grass
then let myself unroll. I am forty.
In ten years I will be fifty and
this yard will be shaded. Now, the heat
is excruciating. The rumble of trucks
and cars floats over across rooftops
from the throughway. It is the Delta and I
am sprawling on my back in copper-colored
dirt after filling sandbags. Through the earth
I feel the kicks of an airstrike that goes on
a klick away. Choppers are wheeling
overhead like hornets. But this
is not a poem about the war.
I'm tired of it always being the war.
This is a poem about how, if I place
my head, that stick of a mulberry tree
in the shape of a Y shades my eyes from the sun.

JOEL OPPENHEIMER

Poem in Defense of Children

liberty to be defended on
foreign shores so that our
children can be safe and free
would seem on the surface to
be reasonable.
　　　　　not one man
who says it will defend his
child himself. let me stand
with a gun at my child's crib,
whose name is the gift of god, the
helpful one, let stand over him
his friends, guardians, parents,
let each opening of his fists,
each start at a smile, each
try at turning over, be covered
by me. it is not my business
that another child burn so
mine shall live. it is not
your business. it is nobody's-
business.
　　　　　or put it this way.
that woman in black pajamas
with babe at breast is evil and
abominable, while my wife with
my child's lips sucking at her
is a holy thing.
　　　　　defend your
homes, your wives and families.

no one else can or will.
                          defend
your lives so that you can
sleep at night. defend your
souls. defend that truth
that is our one inheritance,
or crawl, and cry, and kill.

SIMON J. ORTIZ

War Poem

Oct. 15, Moratorium Day

Santo Domingo, DemRep, March 1965.
I took part, attached
to the 82nd Airborne,
in the U.S. action to "save
the world for democracy."
We landed 35,000 troops
and turned part of Santo Domingo
into rubble and whores.

Acomita, Spring of 1966,
near my home, a couple of nights before
the El Paso Natural Gas Co. line blew up.
The flames towered hundreds of feet upward.
Eulogio Garcia was saying, "I cried.
I got scared. It all came back to me.
I went in my bed when I heard it.
I was there. They told me
I was doing something for my people.
I am telling my children
that it is no good, that it does something
to a man's dignity."
Mr. Garcia, a WWI veteran.

George, a Mexican kid,
wrote me from Vietnam, 1967:
"You know, I feel bad,

this morning I dragged
a boy, V.C., I guess, from a hole.
He was hiding, & he was crying.
The sergeant some punk kid
from Texas kicked him.
I was crying. He looking
like my little brother.
I'm part Indian myself, you know."

Yazzie, young Navajo Vietnam veteran
in Manhattan Bar, 1968, in Gallup.
"I don't know. I don't know."
We watched Nixon on T.V. declare
antiballistics in Montana.
Yazzie's hair still matted with blood.
Got clobbered by the cops.
Just got out of jail. "I don't know."
Shaking his head,
crying onto his Purple Heart.

Acomita, 1968, just off U.S. 66
in the village cemetery.
"He looked so goddam small,
maybe they cut something out of him,
cut him short," said Johnny Poncho
about Jerry Chino's military burial.

Rough Rock, 1969. This morning
I looked out at the flag.
Red and white and blue,
foreign matter whipping in the wind.
The sky is beautiful beyond it.
I think of mountains.
I think of the people.
I think of the harmony possible.

MARK OSAKI

Amnesiac

For awhile I too was haunted by
memories of your frightened faces
as we hovered nearby, shooting
warning tracers above your heads.
It was amazing—you thought waving
American flags would save you.

We had other rooftops to fly to.
Coming back from the last one we
saw the fire you had set as a beacon.
We couldn't help it. We laughed.

The cries and curses you threw up
into that sky were instantly
drowned out and chopped up
by bladed arks already flying away.

I am among my own now, who do not
worship stones or rivers, or impute
to them a memory of any kind.
What does not perish here by forgetting
survives only in the occasional bad dream.

We wake up each morning to a new history.
We don't know if we remember.

BASIL T. PAQUET

They Do Not Go Gentle

The half-dead comatose
Paw the air like cats do when they dream,
They perform isometrics tirelessly.
They flail the air with a vengeance
You know they cannot have.
After all, their multiplication tables,
Memories of momma, and half their id
Lies in some shell hole
Or plop! splatter! on your jungle boots.
It must be some atavistic angst
Of their muscle and bones,
Some ancient ritual of their sea water self,
Some blood stream monsoon,
Some sinew storm that makes
Their bodies rage on tastelessly
Without their shattered brains.

In a Plantation

The bullet passed
Through his right temple,
His left side
Could not hold
Against the metal,
His last "I am" exploded
Red and grey on a rubber tree.

Night Dust-off

A sound like hundreds of barbers
stropping furiously, increases;
suddenly the night lights,
flashing blades thin bodies
into red strips
hunched against the wind
of a settling slickship.

Litters clatter open,
hands reaching
into the dark belly of the ship
touch toward moans,
they are thrust into a privy,
feeling into wounds,
the dark belly all wound,
all wet screams riven limbs
moving in the beaten night.

Basket Case

I waited eighteen years to become a man.
My first woman was a whore off Tu Do street,
But I wish I never felt the first wild
Gliding lust, because the rage and thrust
Of a mine caught me hip high.
I felt the rip at the walls of my thighs,
A thousand metal scythes cut me open,
My little fish shot twenty yards
Into a swamp canal.
I fathered only this—the genderless bitterness

Of two stumps, and an unwanted pity
That births the faces of all
Who will see me till I die deliriously
From the spreading sepsis that was once my balls.

Morning—A Death

Turn—Character 1

I've blown up your chest for thirty minutes
And crushed it down an equal time,
And still you won't warm to my kisses.
I've sucked and puffed on your
Metal No. 8 throat for so long,
And twice you've moaned under my thrusts
On your breastbone. I've worn off
Those sparse hairs you counted noble on your chest,
And twice you defibrillated,
And twice blew back my breath.
I've scanned the rhythms of your living,
Forced half-rhymes in your silent pulse,
Sprung brief spondees in your lungs,
And the caesura's called mid-line, half-time,
Incomplete, but with a certain finality.
The bullet barks apocalyptic
And you don't unzip your sepulchral
Canvas bag in three days.
No rearticulation of nucleics, no phoenix,
No novae, just an arbitrary of one-way bangs
Flowing out to interstitial calms.
The required canonical wait for demotion
To lower order, and you wash out pure chemical.
You are dead just as finally
As your mucosity dries on my lips
In this morning sun.

I have thumped and blown into your kind too often,
I grow tired of kissing the dead.

Counterturn—Character 2

I'd sooner be a fallen pine cone this winter
In a cradle of cold New England rock,
Less hurt in it than nineteen years.
What an exit! Stage left, fronds waving,
Cut down running my ass off at a tree line.
I'm thinking, as I hear my chest
Sucking air through its brand new nipple,
I bought the ticket, I hope I drown fast,
The pain is all in living.

Stand—Character 1

I grow so tired of jostled litters
Filling the racks, and taking off
Your tags and rings, pulling out
Your metal throats and washing
Your spittle down with warm beer at night,
So tired of tucking you all in,
And smelling you all on me for hours.
I'd sooner be in New England this winter
With pine pitch on my hands than your blood,
Lightly fondling breasts and kissing
Women's warm mouths than thumping
Your shattered chests and huffing
In your broken lips or aluminum windpipes,
Sooner lift a straying hair from her wet mouth
Than a tear of elephant grass from your slack lips.
I'd so much rather be making children,
Than tucking so many in.

Easter '68

I have seen the paschal men today.
Long past rising to a passion
they sucked their last sun
through blued lips,
buttressed their intestines in handfuls,
lifting their wounds to the sky
they fell silent as the sun,
as words not spoken,
broken Easters of flesh
girdled in fatigue strips,
red arching rainbows of dead men
rising like a promise
to give Jesus the big kiss
and sinking down—
only my breath on their lips,
only my words on their mouths.

It Is Monsoon at Last

The black peak at Xuan Loc
pulls a red apron of light
up from the east.
105s and 155s are walking shells
toward us from Bear Cat
down some trail
washing a trail in fire.

An eagle flight snakes west toward Lai Khe,
a demonstration of lights
flashing green and red across a sky still black above.

Our boots rattle off the boardwalk
Cha-Chat-Cha-Chat
the sound spills across the helipad
out towards the forest
out towards the dawn;
it chases devil dusters
out to the jungle.

The boardwalk bends
with our ungainly walk
litter handles creak,
with the heavy weight of the dead,
the dull whoosh and thud of B-40s
sounds south along the berm
the quick flat answer of 16s follows.

Gunships are going up
sucking devil dusters into the air.
We can see them through the morgue door
against the red froth clouds
hanging over Xuan Loc.
We lift the boy into a death bag.
We lift the boy into the racks.
We are building a bunker of dead.
We are stacking the dead for protection.

This dead boy is on my hands
My thighs are wet with the vomit of death
His blood is on my mouth
My mouth My mouth tastes his blood.

The gunships are firing over the Dong Nai
throwing fire into the river
clouds are coming in from the sea
I can smell the rain, see it
over Xuan Loc, over me
it is monsoon at last.

Graves Registration

From the trucks we see
the black shark fin of Xuan Loc
break from the swelling green sea jungle,
cutting the thick red air of dusk.
The sound of the engines washes
into the gullies of heaped wire
strung with bodies spilling toward the village
like a trail of crushed sea forms.
Great fish-mountain
did you show your grin here?
Did your face break surface,
mouth of magnificent death?
The tank shells are like popped cans,
their meat turning in the sun.
Carapace, claws, antennae—
debris all stiff with death
and swelled by the panting sun,
what are we to do with you?

"Too many. We'll get another truck."

"Fuck the gooks. We'll use lime."

"Kipper, stay with the bodies!"

The land cannot hold you all,
it is filling with debris.
We will have to ship some home
for recycling.
When the truck comes back
we will wrap you in plastic—zip! zip!
You brown-yellow guys

are going to get some whiteness,
you're going home to Xuan Loc "passing."
Rotting into the earth in dusted rows,
seeping into the earth in chemicals,
your moisture already lifting into the air
to rub the dark fin in night mists,
to cover us with your breath
while we lie drunken in our camps.

This morning you all
must have been violent!
Strung out along this road
like tatters on the wire
you seem a strange attack.
I heard your noise in the early darkness
from my hootch,
I toasted your anarchy with gin.
Did you all think death?
Did you speak in whispers
or shout at war
in quick metal breath?
Did you shout at death,
or did he glide into your mouths
while you sucked some J's?

"The brightness of sun
caught this morning
in his red fist
the smashed flowers
of our faces,
licked the wetness
the drying surprise   "Something crushed my
from our petal-eyes   face. I was thinking of
and reeled on."   freedom and hunger."

"I used to salty dog
and tongue with laughter
soft brown breast heads."

* * *

"The sky trod us in walking shells,
our eyes shallow pools
for the tongues of flies
and a thirsty sun."
"I remember a cloud
against the flares.
I was high as a mother.
it looked like a fish."

"We are the ripped
forest,
men who became
the jungle,
limed limbs
whitening,
silent as the
mountain,
as the last seal of
lips."

"Laughter shredded in my mouth.
I felt my throat rip in a choke,
the earth heaved with flame."

"Tonight the paleness of moon will
light on our stilled limbs,
flutter with clouds,
and fly to deeper night
with carrion of our dreams."

"The beast moved among us,
our voices hurled back
by the fire,
we fell silent, unhurried
as the whorl
on stiff red fingertips."

Why do I move among you
like a berserk ballerina,
tippy-toeing over you
filling out your tags
and powdering the rest?

I cannot believe anymore
that names count.
I fear some day
the beast will come for me,
but that we will rush
to each other like lovers,
secret sharers in the memory of your passing.
Even more I fear that
some day
I will be the only one remembering.

I wish you could share this
joint with me.

The trucks will be back soon.

Mourning the Death, by Hemorrhage, of a Child from Honai

Always the children are included
In these battles for the body politic.
Prefaced with mortars and rockets
The Year of the Monkey was preluded
By the mephitic
Stench of blasted bodies sullenly drifting from the
     pocket

Of refugee hootches at Honai.
The enemy patriots knew the young
Would be glad to die for the revolution.
The allies were certain the vox populi
Called a mandate for flag-strung
Counterattack and awful retribution.

The majesty of the annihilation of the city
Could be heard clearly in the background,

225

I could only wonder what ideology
The child carried in her left arm—necessity
Must have dictated an M-16 round
Should cut it off, and her gaining the roll of
    martyrology.

Her dying in my arms, this daughter
Weaned on war, was for the greater
Glory of all concerned.
There was no time to mourn your slaughter
Small, denuded, one-armed thing, I too was violator,
And after the first death, the many must go
    unmourned.

Group Shot

So they passed,
Days of hollow cadence
When each passing day
Seemed an album of daguerreotypes,
Camera-caught, anachronistic.
Puffed-up, pigeon-breasted,
As in Brady's day
We strutted to a distant
Very insistent drum.

I have photos of us all together,
Polished boots and brass
In front of whitewashed barracks.
There, hanging on the parlor wall,
We are as once we were,
The wholeness of our limbs,
·Two eyes blinking at the sun,
When all had all needed
To woo the world.

ANTHONY PETROSKY

V.A. Hospital

in memory of John Makstutis

Yesterday I didn't know this place.
Today I wished you were dead.

The hallways are hollow drum logs.
This is the white history of death:
TV, cigarettes, magazines,
all the stupid charities
cluttered on a table.

I am the stranger here.
I have never seen a man alive with his face cut off
as clean as steel below his eyes.
In the name of Christ, how do you live?
Is it the gray spiders clinging
to your eyes that keep you alive?

My own guilt clings to your eyes.
In a dream, I hear the echoes of women
pounding these halls to love you.

From the outside I bring nothing of use.

JOHN CLARK PRATT

Words and *Thoughts*

Hey, you, *you slant-eyed, luscious brown-skinned*
    broad,
Why you no smile tonight? What you no hab?
Where your zoomie tealoch-man who keep you,
Pay you, love you? He butterfly around again?

Maybe he go home States and send for you.
Big joke. It neber hoppen. He buddy me.
He hot jet jockey, sure, but he hab wife,
Three baby-san. He short-time. He speak lie.

No worry, babes, no sweat. I tell you true.
You have long legs, great calves, soft, rounded thighs.
You need no Hongkong bra. You number One.
You nice girl. You not nit-noy. You super-Thai.

I same-same. No hab mama-san like him.
You be my tealoch, I extend a year.
I make love good—always use balloon.
I long time love you mach mach—chai?

Don't cry, please. I'm sorry. I no try
To hurt you. I just make damn silly joke.
I'm just a pilot, very far from home.
Me number Ten. Very dumb GI.

Your tealoch good man. Marry you someday.

Please, what's the matter? What you say?
He shot down? He work Tchepone today?
I didn't know. Flew last night. Slept all day.

You loved that part of him he let you love, I know.
But so did we.
Please stop your crying and forgive us all,
As well as me.

DON RECEVEUR

Night Fear

i heard my meatless bones
clunk together
saw the ants drink
from my eyes
like red ponies
at brown pools of water
and the worms in my belly
moved sluggishly
delighted.

August 17, 1970

We dug up a
grave today.
It was next
to a caved in
bunker,
deep in
the underbrush.
The bones showed
disease yellow
through the rags
and the skull
was covered with
ants,
like medals

on a colonel's chest.
They told us
to.
They said it might
contain something
of military importance.

Doper's Dream

The mind
becomes an
oil-slicked pool
of night time
liquid,
under the oil
dark shapes
struggle and mate,
small still-born
terrors
rise toward the surface.

Eagle in the Land of Oz

i was talking
to a friend
and i noticed
a tin
leg
            hanging on his wall
he said he
got it
            in cambodia
there had been

CARRYING THE DARKNESS

an air strike
on a
          n.v.a. hospital
it had been on
one
          of the bodies
i thought of the
Tin Man of Oz
          who had no heart
lions and tigers and bears.

DALE RITTERBUSCH

Search and Destroy

They came out of the hootch
with their hands up—surrendered—
and we found all that rice
and a couple of weapons. They
were tagged and it all seemed so easy—
too easy, and someone started to torch
the hootch and I stopped him—something
was funny. We checked the hootch
a couple times more; I had them probe it
like we were searching for mines and
a lucky poke with a knife
got us the entrance to a tunnel.
We didn't wait for any damn
tunnel clearers—we threw down
CS and smoke and maybe two hundred
yards to our right two gooks popped up
and we got 'em running across the field,
nailed 'em before they hit the trees.
We went to the other hole and popped more
gas and smoke and a fragmentation grenade
and three gooks came out coughing, tears
and red smoke pouring out of their eyes and
nose. We thought there were more
so we threw in another grenade and one of the
dinks brought down his arms, maybe he started
to sneeze with all that crap running out of his face,
maybe he had a weapon concealed, I didn't know,
so I greased him. Wasn't much else I could do.
A sudden move like that.

LARRY ROTTMANN

APO 96225

A young man once went off to war
in a far country.
When he had time, he wrote home and
said, "Sure rains here a lot."

But his mother, reading between the lines,
Wrote, "We're quite concerned. Tell us
what it's really like."

And the young man responded, "Wow, you ought
to see the funny monkeys!"

To which the mother replied, "Don't
hold back, how is it?"

And the young man wrote, "The sunsets here
are spectacular."

In her next letter the mother
wrote, "Son we want you to tell us
everything."

So the next time he wrote,
"Today I killed a man.
Yesterday I helped drop napalm on women and
children. Tomorrow we are going to use
gas."

* * *
And the father wrote, "Please don't
write such depressing letters. You're upsetting
your mother."

So, after a while, the young man wrote, "Sure rains a
lot here . . ."

VERN RUTSALA

The Silence

Ohio, Winter 1970

Every day is a long pause without seams,
the world empty, winter everywhere,
cracked puddles like broken bowls
and the flat scuffed land

going in all directions on its belly.
Language gone featureless as numbers
one word is like another as a branch
stiff as bone scrapes its fingernail

across the kitchen window. After midnight now
I hear train whistles and braking wheels
that seem to carry sobs and wild lost
cries at the crossing up the street.

There is the squeal of slaughtered animals
and tires and the dead fields whispering:
curl up, a wind is coming; curl up, no one
will notice; curl up, the only way

to stay alive is to lie still as death.

JOHN C. SCHAFER

Battle Lines

Now you've learned not to let your eyes
Rest too long on a yellow face,
Or allow them to reveal yourself
Too much, too soon, with too much joy
Or gentle interest, or hope laid bare
For a friendly word or things to share.

Now you've grown painfully aware
That the long unhurried look,
Rich in promises of a world to share,
Was a luxury of another place
And time, and now you know how rare
That way of looking always was.

Now you know a look can seem a stare;
No matter how quick or kind the glance,
Or even if your eyes should meet by chance
The face sets and the awful sneer is there;
The lips like battle lines are drawn,
And it's too late to talk of things to share.

And all the while you force yourself to see
That the hatred and quiet disdain,
Are for what you represent, and the pain
From other times when he like you began
His looks with hope, felt the pain,
And learned not to make that mistake again.

CARRYING THE DARKNESS

* * *

The surprise is not the people's hate
But that those lines etched in armored plate
Do ever break, can ever soften
Into something like a smile;
And hands still reach across the breach
For things more warm than charity.

RICHARD SHELTON

Eden After Dark

today
must have been Sunday
all the flowers were closed

the river which brought us
news of the battle
has been chained to its bed

even under torture
the map refuses to name names

the words we saved
for an emergency are gone
leaving us
with the terrible irony of gestures
which should have been made

in a paradise of burned bridges
the sadness is everywhere
we are already tired
of the war and there is
so much killing left to be done

we have given up sleep
at night we close our eyes quickly
and fall forward
into the arms of despair

JOSEPH A. SOLDATI

Surroundings

A letter from my brother
Unlike any other:
They are tearing up our early surroundings, Sol,
Going are the houses, our house,
The wide shade from the walks,
The alleys of our early talks.
They are taking away the morning
Clip-clop of the ice-wagon mule,
And maybe the morning too.

You were five, I was three
In nineteen forty-four, and we
Destroyed a Ford with half a brick,
An antique chair with just one kick,
And I can't remember who pushed who
In the wagon through the porch glass.
Long trains were going to Asia then,
And still are.
Two small boys,
Who rushed to see them pass, are men—
Have been there and come home again.

Alone, I opened the closet beneath the stairs,
Acknowledged the demons dwelling there,
And left them to scare our ghosts along.
Lost, I closed the door that had seemed so strong,
Walked once around the house-embracing porch,
And was gone.
John.

WILLIAM STAFFORD

Report from an Unappointed Committee

The uncounted are counting
  and the unseen are looking around.

In a room of northernmost light
  a sculptor is waiting.

In some university a strict experiment
  has indicated a need for
    more strict experiments.

A wild confusion of order is clawing through
  a broken system of our most reliable wires.

In the farthest province a comet
  has flamed in the gaze of
    an unofficial watcher.

In the back country a random raindrop
  has broken a dam.

And a new river is out feeling for a valley
  somewhere under our world.

MICHAEL STEPHENS

After Asia

Her poets die for the mountains,
where my tears are only for a people
far away, far out, in the far east,
rice in the sea, curds in the mouth,
taste her seaweed in this hot sauce,
magpie in the pine, courtyard of rock
and stone, soldiers in the treeline,
president assassinated in the night,
martial cadenzas, unreachable,
unbelievable, I wake and say it only
was a dream, but then I walk and say,
this is not a dream, I am in Asia,
their soldiers, our soldiers, the others
across the demilitarized zone
where the rarest of birds habitate,
every haircut gets a shave with a straight-
edged razor, they massage your heels
and unzip you, and when they cut your throat
it is erotic, give me beer, give me wine,
let me see the breasts of Asia's women,
let her poets die in the mountains
or have their tongues cut out
in the granite cells of the prison,
after Asia you can call me a man.

The Carp

As a carp ascends to heaven,
The moon rises through the corn husks
And water in the rice field
Turns to silver; the poplars shimmer
In the moonlight like quilled pens
And the tawny owl hoos of summer.
The carp ascends to heaven, breaking
Through the smoky surface of night water,
Bursting upward like a scaled jet—
By morning it becomes a dragon.

FRANK STEWART

Black Winter

. . . for a coming time . . . the boys have memories.

JEFFERS

1

The time between us stretches out
like a winter, lingering farther from the heart,
heavy as fourteen thousand miles of jet and rails.
Looking out, I can't tell whether the glass is crusted
with frost or if the land is beyond it, a white
face of resistance. The train from Malmo thrashes
the butcher-cold sleepers, drives me through the
gut of frozen landscape like a knife. Deep fog
so early. Us. Where can we meet anyone now except
on the edge of ice, anywhere so long as it isn't a jungle.

2

They said that Stockholm would make mortician
slabs of us American boys, cold and rootless. In
Montreal the summer before, underground
looking east and north, I met Charles X with you.
"Bright California black boy. He'll get everything
   right
in Sweden." And at first he was a fad in Lund, you
said, easy to get dates, domestic jobs like we all
needed. Then the exile's disease, common guilts,
assault, journalist's ink. Lost the same as if
in a jungle, you said. Everyday the papers full

of butchery. "Oriental rubbish swept into a
pile by black & white GIs." But here she's sweet,
he'd say. "She's Swedish pastry. No war and sweet
times." Someone else's car, six months into exile, a
yellow piece of dress, black billows, and just
small, American, Black rubbish on the ice.

3

First night we sat and watched the Swedish hospital
   burn,
bullhorn, glare of fire, lights, long engines—
imagining a jungle we'd both escaped beyond
   Honolulu.
"Exiles should stay out of the sun," you said
   laughing,
our breasts cold and tight so far north even self-
preservation froze. "Along the circle, the Lapps dance
and chant stories through half a year of night, not
for entertainment but to keep from going crazy in the
darkness." The survivors here are fractured like cold
glass, bits of ghost in ice and heavy smoke. Wet, black
winter's going out. No one talks of escape.

4

Out by the reef a low fire is burning on the sea,
and in the silent dark a color like old roses
is shining on the swells. When they'd burn off
the cover in those green jungles, the suffocating
small hills would crouch there beyond the flames
like these waves. Ten years beyond the war on this
wharf, I can justify almost nothing so simply as this
fire. The smell of petroleum burning and brine slams
me like a fist that strikes on a cold morning
and strikes again, insists and strikes until there's only
blood and burning through the nostrils. A black
mirror: "One should watch and not speak. And
   patriotism

has run the world through so many blood-lakes: and
we always fall in . . .''

5
Near the far horizon the fire is out. The stars
blink on again through heavy smoke. The Pacific sea
extends again into space. And who did we leave
in the north like ice, and who did we leave there
in the south, scattered on the land like coal?

BILL TREMBLAY

Mayday

for Richard M. Nixon

I saw police biting corktip cigarettes
as reports of cars burning in Georgetown
crackled through their radios

    the sky so crisp D.C. blue
    & the grass' piercing green meant this was it

       & when we threw construction beams
       into Constitution Avenue they roared off
       Capitol Hill, sirens happy now

scattering us every which way
motorcycle cops ran us down on sidewalks
& above helicopters guttered like spider gods.

    At the Mall where the Washington Monument
    wanted to fall, the ultimate nightstick
    on Dr Spock's head, squad cars tore up
    shooting teargas in smoky arcs.

Everyone was swallowed by buses.
Cops wore elephant-face gasmasks & hid their badges,
laughing, *What a piece of cake!*
               *
A guard pressed the button
& we descend through layers of the brain.

247

Violet fingerprints, flashbulb blindness
clothes still frying from the CS.
The cell door's clang, their blot of finality.

"Give me liberty or give me dope!" someone
shouted.
"You guards better get us some dope
& get it here quick. You ever seen 3000 crazy
hippies goin' cold turkey!"

But as the hours melted the shouting
the ancient games of prisoner & jailer came
out.

"Don't you have any feelings for the people
being napalmed & killed?"

"Yeah, I got me a feeling. To re-up
so's I can get me back to Nam & gut a slant."

"Would you gut me?"

"Depends on if you're raisin' hell ag'in.
I'd as soon gut a chickenshit pacifist
as a charlie, so remember,
I'm studyin' on your face right now."

Endless dead light. Somehow
the smell of hot tar the guards' faces
are smeared with, marking them as creatures of this
place.

Then the stories.
The ex-Marine who flipped on a carrier
in the South China Sea rapping about "green
plexiglas maps shining in the wardrooms
dividing the world & bird colonels crying
in their psycho ward cells at Quonset"

* * *

another one tripping his brains out muttering
"You want me to cut my foot off;
I won't do it. You want me to eat bleached
bread; I won't do it. You want me
to be your guillotine; I won't do it."

Silence got us.
We would have promised to go back to grass
& cultivate a shrunken head & cut our hair & never
    raise hell
again to smell free air.

* *

Released on PR
I wandered the lettered streets alone
thinking of that mechanical gorge
in Islip, Long Island, compressing the bodies
of burned automobiles & men with black lunchpails
walking to work with the dust
which drove them from Utah swirling inside them,
saw the one-horse towns where their mothers
dreamed the silver screen & no one laughed
no one gossiped on ice-box porches, all
the women holding their breasts to electric fans
demanding magic, more magic, nothing but magic.

saw a man in the center of a prairie
listening to darkness & then people by the
    millions
filling up the land with ploughshares, horses
the noise of lust, scarlet fever & self-sacrifice,
saw tumbleweed rule the empty streets.

Even as I looked over my shoulder for squad cars
quaking with the thought of being dragged
back down there I thought
if that man could touch the vanishing point
his town & children get born out of
& die into

* * *

if he could wheelwright the wagon
of his own dreams, asking hawks or mesquite
how to pass out of or into the light
in his rags of song

it wouldn't be this way,
people killing each other
on the way to the Seven Cities of Gold,
it could be beans, squash, corn &
    thanksgiving,
bells striking angelus
in the parish of the world.

Home Front

for Cynthia

Handing out anti-war leaflets at United Aircraft
I shouted, "Learn what the jets you build
are used for!" A Black held up his paycheck.
"This here's the most I ever made in my life.
I got mouths to feed at home."

At home I wanted you to sympathize.
All those hours trying to teach a wider world.

You were busy with Ben.
Two years sick, he was a thin ghost.
Your spoon plane was trying to come in
for the thousandth unhappy landing into his mouth
with all he could digest—the same rice cereal
as yesterday & the day before, *ad nauseam.*

Tonight, remembering those days
I also remember my father say to my mother

in the three-decker kitchen of my childhood
"He better do good in school, Irene,
him born blind like that even with the operation
he's damaged goods, he'll never do a man's work."

I'd hear Ben coming & think "he's damaged goods
    too"
& couldn't bear to look at him.

This has nothing to do with the others
& why they tried to stop the war.
This has to do with when I stopped trying
to stop the war & went home.

TOM WAYMAN

Despair

*DOW appears, and the poet Robert Bly, and a
building is taken and lost November 1968*

1

As though something knew Bly was coming
the night he arrived the first snow began
to sigh wearily down on
the building we argued in
down on the humps in the parked streets,
on houses.
At the edge of town: cold fields
where we found sadness in cabin lights
being forced unhappily out onto the white ground.
We loaded the truck with black boards for
barricades, from the floor of an old silo,
breathing the new winter around us
whispering, whispering down resigned
to the state of things, to itself;
to America, Bly and to quiet.

2

In the black hall of the building
crash of boards dropped, pools of melting snow
and light here and there from passageways.
Hammers. The janitor being talked to upstairs.
We move through the rooms, jam
boards to hold doors tight, lock the big windows,
nail others shut,

slide out the classroom chairs to be
piled one by one against entrances,
tighten wire across wood that could move
to let in the day. But into the flickering noise:
doubts.
"This place is a sieve, we'll never hold it."
"If the police come now or come early
this handful of us is lost for nothing."
And is this where your life changes, your job goes
to another town, the spectre of clubs and gas,
shoving helmets and jail?
The building slows; some faces drift in the hall:
"The place is a sieve, we'll never hold it."
"If we had three hundred instead of thirty, we
   could. . . ."
"Let's just leave the blockades and go."
Some others go past in the darkness, carrying
a heavy plank.

Again in the open air, I want to learn
depths of commitment or cowardice
crossing the empty streets with some others
to the cold car. What does this leaving mean?
Black flashes of levering a huge partition
against some windows, slumping to a chair,
   considering:
where does your life change, if not here. Maybe
nothing will happen. What then, but to have learned
what you would do or not do? Footsteps
on the snowy sidewalk leading into the building.
Footsteps out on the ice in the early, early morning.

3
So of all of us who began, fifteen are in custody by
   noon.
And Bly in the afternoon speaks softly
of a great despair in the land: like the deep snow
out of the lounge windows where he talks, easing down

on the hills and frozen trees. Only fifteen left and
   willing
to face the massed police and be busted, and Bly
speaks of them slowly, waving his red wristband of
   support
for the Milwaukee Fourteen, who napalmed draft
   records
months ago on cement in the sunshine. Bly in the
   evening
sighs as a wind, his sweet voice soothing
and crackling like a gentle fire in a grate somewhere
warm against a cold night, saying how much
America longs to sleep, longs to forget its Empire
and the wars of Empire, the hatred of all the men of the
   world
it can burn but not own. Sleep! Bly cries. Sleep.
And in jail, the others say later, it was too cold
to sleep, but I nod in the back of the theatre
mumbling yes, yes
I would love sleep, an end to this testing myself
and my words against plans, against actions, afraid
in movements and struggle where love and trust
are not born yet, too new, too beaten by fear,
guilt, doubt. Sleep, and an end to optimism
trying to cheer myself and perhaps another
with the anecdotes of history: with a certainty and
joy that escaped me, it seems,
in the past night when the bitter bone
of a sure defeat seemed worthless
compared to running away to the daily reverses of
talk. Bly, the winter, and slumber swirl in as a fog
of despair at myself, my retreat from myself.
Where am I now in Colorado?
There is so much snow.

Teething

In the dark house, the cry of a child.
Her teeth are trying to be born:
the tiny incisors
are cutting their way up
through flesh, into a mouth
now open and crying.

Deep snow around the house
beside the forest. Indoors, in the night
the sleepy voice of the mother, then the father,
and the child's steady crying.
All at once the father is up, and a moment later
he brings the child into another room
and sits in an old rocker.

The noise of the chair starts
as its wooden dowels and slats
adjust repeatedly to the weight being swung
back and forth. The chair moves
not with the easy pace
of someone assured, experienced,
but with the urgent drive of a young man
rocking and rocking. The chair creaks
persistently, determinedly,
like the sound of boots on the snowy road outside
in the day, going somewhere.

                But it is here
the father has come to. In the dark room, in the chair
ten years as an adult pass, the chair
rocks out a decade of meetings, organizations, sit-ins.
It rocks out Chicago, and Cook County jail.

It rocks out any means necessary
to end the War, fight racism, abolish the draft.
It rocks out grad school and marriage.
It rocks out Cambodia, and at last
jobs, a new country, and a child.

But the chair

falls back each time
to the centre of things, so it also rocks back
all these lives up into these lives: the father
rocking
with his child in his arms
at the edge of sleep. In the still house at Salmon Arm
the sound of the rocking chair
in the winter night. Sudden cry of the child.
Cry of the world.

RON WEBER

A Concise History of
the Vietnam War: 1965–1968

The air in the room is dark and greasy
as a city slicker's hair. LBJ reaches out
and finds what he wants. The balls are small,
easily cupped in his hand. So he knows
he's right when he says, "I've got Ho
where I want him. I've got the bastard
by the nuts and I won't let go
till he yells uncle." It is only later,
after Lyndon gets blue in the face,
that he knows he's made a mistake.

BRUCE WEIGL

Sailing to Bien Hoa

In my dream of the hydroplane
I'm sailing to Bien Hoa
the shrapnel in my thighs
like tiny glaciers.
I remember a flower,
a kite, a mannikin playing the guitar,
a yellow fish eating a bird, a truck
floating in urine, a rat carrying a banjo,
a fool counting the cards, a monkey praying,
a procession of whales, and far off
two children eating rice,
speaking French—
I'm sure of the children,
their damp flutes,
the long line of their vowels.

Surrounding Blues on the Way Down

I was barely in country. December, hot,
We slipped under rain black clouds
Opening around us like orchids.
He'd come to take me into the jungle
So I felt the loneliness
Though I did not yet hate the beautiful war.
Eighteen years old and a man

Was telling me how to stay alive
In the tropics he said would rot me—

Brothers of the heart he said and smiled
Until we came upon a mama san
Bent over from her stuffed sack of flowers.
We flew past her
But he hit the brakes hard,
He spun the tires backwards in the mud.
He did not hate the war either
But other reasons made him cry out to her
So she stopped,
She smiled her beetle black teeth at us,
She raised her arms in the air.

I have no excuse for myself,
I sat in that man's jeep in the rain
And watched him slam her to her knees,
The plastic butt of his M-16
Crashing down on her.
I was barely in country, the clouds
Hung like huge flowers, black
Like her teeth.

Girl at the Chu Lai Laundry

All this time I had forgotten.
My miserable platoon was moving out
One day in the war and I had my clothes in the laundry.
I ran the two dirt miles.
Convoy already forming behind me. I hit
The block of small hooches and saw her
Twist out the black rope of her hair in the sun.
She did not look up at me,
Not even when I called to her for my clothes.

She said I couldn't have them,
They were wet. . . .

Who would've thought the world stops
Turning in the war, the tropical heat like hate
And your platoon moves out without you,
Your wet clothes piled
At the feet of the girl at the laundry,
Beautiful with her facts.

Mines

1

In Vietnam I was always afraid of mines:
North Vietnamese mines, Vietcong mines,
French mines, American mines,
whole fields marked with warning signs.

A Bouncing Betty comes up waist high—
cuts you in half.
One man's legs were laid
alongside him in the Dustoff,
he asked for a chairback, morphine,
he screamed he wanted to give
his eyes away, his kidneys,
his heart . . .

2

Here is how you walk at night: slowly lift
one leg, clear the sides with your arms, clear the back,
front, put the leg down, like swimming.

Temple Near Quang Tri, Not on the Map

Dusk, the ivy thick with sparrows
Squawking for more room
Is all we hear; we see
Birds move on the walls of the temple
Shaping their calligraphy of wings.
Ivy is thick in the grottoes,
On the moon-watching platform
And ivy keeps the door from fully closing.

The point man leads us and we are
Inside, lifting
The white wash bowl, the smaller bowl
For rice, the stone lanterns
And carved stone heads that open
Above the carved faces for incense.
But even the bamboo sleeping mat
Rolled in the corner,
Even the place of prayer is clean.
And a small man

Sits legs askew in the shadow
The farthest wall casts
Halfway across the room.
He is bent over, his head
Rests on the floor, and he is speaking something
As though to us and not to us.
The CO wants to ignore him;
He locks and loads and fires a clip into the walls
Which are not packed with rice this time
And tells us to move out.

* * *

But one of us moves towards the man,
Curious about what he is saying.
We bend him to sit straight up
And when he is nearly peaked
At the top of his slow uncurling
His face becomes visible, his eyes
Roll down to the charge
Wired between his chin and the floor.
The sparrows
Burst off the walls into the jungle.

The Sharing

I have not ridden a horse much,
two, maybe three times,
a broken gray mare my cousin called Ghost.
Then only in the fall
through the flat pastures of Ohio.
That's not much,
but I watched two Chinese tanks
roll out of the jungle side by side,
their turret guns feeling before them
like a man walking through his dream,
their tracks slapping the bamboo like hooves.

I can't name the gaits of a horse
except the canter,
and that rocks you high to the withers,
but I saw those arms,
those guns and did not know for a moment
what they were, but knew they were not horses
as they pulled themselves deep
into the triple-canopy jungle
until there was only the dull rattle of their tracks

and a boy on a gray horse,
flying through the opening fields.

The Ambassador

Bunker the ambassador. Does Bunker have a bunker?
He must have a bunker with chrome faucets and a
sauna. They must call it: Mr. Bunker's bunker.
He must be shaking his head.

Burning Shit at An Khe

Into that pit
　　I had to climb down
With a rake and matches; eventually,
　　You had to do something
Because it just kept piling up
　　And it wasn't our country, it wasn't
Our air thick with the sick smoke
　　So another soldier and I
Lifted the shelter off its blocks
　　To expose the homemade toilets:
Fifty-five gallon drums cut in half
　　With crude wood seats that splintered.
We soaked the piles in fuel oil
　　And lit the stuff
And tried to keep the fire burning.
　　To take my first turn
I paid some kid
　　A care package of booze from home.
I'd walked past the burning once
　　And gagged the whole heart of myself—
It smelled like the world

CARRYING THE DARKNESS

    Was on fire,
But when my turn came again
    There was no one
So I stuffed cotton up my nose
    And marched up that hill. We poured
And poured until it burned and black
    Smoke curdled
But the fire went out.
    Heavy artillery
Hammered the evening away in the distance,
    Vietnamese laundry women watched
From a safe place, laughing.
    I'd grunted out eight months
Of jungle and thought I had a grip on things
    But we flipped the coin and I lost
And climbed down into my fellow soldiers'
    Shit and began to sink and didn't stop
Until I was deep to my knees. Liftships
    Cut the air above me, the hacking
Blast of their blades
    Ripped dust in swirls so every time
I tried to light a match
    It died
And it all came down on me, the stink
    And the heat and the worthlessness
Until I slipped and climbed
    Out of that hole and ran
Past the olive drab
    Tents and trucks and clothes and everything
Green as far from the shit
    As the fading light allowed.
Only now I can't fly.
    I lie down in it
And finger paint the words of who I am
    Across my chest
Until I'm covered and there's only one smell,
    One word.

Song for the Lost Private

The night we were to meet in the hotel
In the forbidden Cholon district
You didn't show
So I drank myself into a filthy
Room with a bar girl
Who had terrible scars
She ran her fingers over
As we bartered for the night.
But drunk I couldn't do anything, angry
I threw the mattress to the street
And stood out on the balcony naked,
Cursing your name to the night.
She thought I was crazy and tried to give my money
    back.
I don't know how to say I tried again,
I saw myself in the mirror and couldn't move.
She crushed the paper money in her fist
And curled in sleep away from me
So I felt cruel, cold, and small arms fire
Cracked in the marketplace below.
I thought I heard you call back my name
But white flares lit the sky
Casting the empty streets in clean light
And the firing stopped.
I couldn't sleep so I touched her
Small shoulders, traced the curve of her spine,
Traced the scars,
The miles we were all from home.

Him, on the Bicycle

There was no light; there was no light at all . . .
ROETHKE

In a liftship near Hue
the door gunner is in a trance.
He's that driver who falls
asleep at the wheel
between Pittsburgh and Cleveland
staring at the Ho Chi Minh trail.

Flares fall,
where the river leaps
I go stiff,
I have to think, tropical.

The door gunner sees movement,
the pilot makes small circles:
four men running, carrying rifles,
one man on a bicycle.

He pulls me out of the ship,
there's firing far away.
I'm on the back of the bike
holding his hips.
It's hard pumping for two,
I hop off and push the bike.

I'm brushing past trees,
the man on the bike stops pumping,
lifts his feet,
we don't waste a stroke.
His hat flies off,

I catch it behind my back,
put it on, I want to live forever!

Like a blaze
streaming down the trail.

Anna Grasa

I came home from Vietnam.
My father had a sign
made at the foundry:
WELCOME HOME BRUCE
in orange glow paint.
He rented spotlights,
I had to squint.
WELCOME HOME BRUCE.

Out of the car I moved
up on the sign
dreaming myself full,
the sign that cut the sky,
my eyes burned.

But behind the terrible thing
I saw my grandmother,
beautiful Anna Grasa.
I couldn't tell her, tell her.

I clapped to myself,
clapped to the sound of her dress.
I could have put it on
she held me so close,
both of us could be inside.

Monkey

Out of the horror there rises a musical ache that is
beautiful . . .

JAMES WRIGHT

1

I am you are he she it is
they are you are we are.
I am you are he she it is
they are you are we are.
When they ask for your number
pretend to be breathing.
Forget the stinking jungle,
force your fingers between the lines.
Learn to get out of the dew.
The snakes are thirsty.
Bladders, water, boil it, drink it.
Get out of your clothes:
you can't move in your green clothes.
Your O.D. in color issue.
Get out the plates and those who ate,
those who spent the night.
Those small Vietnamese soldiers.
They love to hold your hand.
Back away from their dark cheeks.
Small Vietnamese soldiers.
They love to love you.
I have no idea how it happened,
I remember nothing but light.

2

I don't remember the hard
swallow of the lover.

I don't remember the burial of ears.
I don't remember
the time of the explosion.
This is the place curses are manufactured:
delivered like white tablets.
The survivor is spilling his bedpan.
He slips a curse into your pocket,
you're finally satisfied.
I don't remember the heat
in the hands,
the heat around the neck.

Good times bad times sleep
get up work. Sleep get up
good times bad times.
Work eat sleep good bad work times.
I like a certain cartoon of wounds.
The water which refused to dry.
I like a little unaccustomed mercy.
Pulling the trigger is all we have.
I hear a child.

3

I dropped to the bottom of a well.
I have a knife.
I cut someone with it.
Oh, I have the petrified eyebrows
of my Vietnam monkey.
My monkey from Vietnam.
My monkey.
Put your hand here.
It makes no sense.
I beat the monkey.
I didn't know him.
He was bloody.
He lowered his intestines
to my shoes. My shoes
spit-shined the moment

I learned to tie the bow.
I'm not on speaking terms
with anyone. In the wrong climate
a person can spoil,
the way a pair of boots slows you down. . . .

I don't know when I'm sleeping.
I don't know if what I'm saying
is anything at all.
I'll lie on my monkey bones.

4
I'm tired of the rice
falling in slow motion
like eggs from the smallest animal.
I'm twenty-five years old,
quiet, tired of the same mistakes,
the same greed, the same past.
The same past with its bleat
and pound of the dead,
with its hand grenade
tossed into a hootch on a dull Sunday
because when a man dies like that
his eyes sparkle,
his nose fills with witless nuance
because a farmer in Bong Son
has dead cows lolling
in a field of claymores
because the VC tie hooks to their comrades
because a spot of blood
is a number
because a woman is lifting
her dress across the big pond.

If we're soldiers we should smoke them
if we have them. Someone's bound
to point us in the right direction
sooner or later.

* * *

I'm tired and I'm glad you asked.

5

There is a hill.
Men run top hill.
Men take hill.
Give hill to man.

*

Me and my monkey
and me and my monkey
my Vietnamese monkey
my little brown monkey
came with me
to Guam and Hawaii
in Ohio he saw
my people he
jumped on my daddy
he slipped into mother
he baptized my sister
he's my little brown monkey
he came here from heaven
to give me his spirit imagine
my monkey my beautiful
monkey he saved me lifted
me above the punji
sticks above the mines
above the ground burning
above the dead above
the living above the
wounded dying the wounded
dying.

* *

Men take hill away from smaller men.
Men take hill and give to fatter man.
Men take hill. Hill has number.
Men run up hill. Run down.

Mercy

Enough snow over last night's ice
So the road appears safe, appears
As a long white scar unfolding.
Ohio, cold
Hawk off Lake Erie
And only enough light to see vague outlines:
The castle-like shape of mill stacks
And the shape of gulls' wings
Dipping to the parking lot for garbage
Lashed this way and that by the wind
These nights have in common.
I pumped gas from five to midnight
For minimum wage
Because I had a family and the war
Made me stupid, and only dead enough
To clean windshields.
When you clean the windshields of others
You see your own face
Reflected in the glass.
I looked and saw only enough hope
To lift me car to car and in between
I breathed the oil smell and the fly strips
And the vending candy air.
The *Gulf* sign clanged in the gale,
The plate glass strained like a voice
I thought would shatter
Yet still cars came: dim headlights
Casting the snow
Into a silver sheet,
Then the fenders like low clouds,
Then the bundled families
And the hushed sound

When father opened the window
And slipped me the money for gas.
Only a second when our eyes catch
And the wind shows some mercy.

Song of Napalm

for my wife

After the storm, after the rain stopped pounding,
We stood in the doorway watching horses
Walk off lazily across the pasture's hill.
We stared through the black screen,
Our vision altered by the distance
So I thought I saw a mist
Kicked up around their hooves when they faded
Like cut-out horses
Away from us.
The grass was never more blue in that light, more
Scarlet; beyond the pasture
Trees scraped their voices into the wind, branches
Crisscrossed the sky like barbed wire
But you said they were only branches.

Okay. The storm stopped pounding.
I am trying to say this straight: for once
I was sane enough to pause and breathe
Outside my wild plans and after the hard rain
I turned my back on the old curses. I believed
They swung finally away from me . . .

But still the branches are wire
And thunder is the pounding mortar,
Still I close my eyes and see the girl
Running from her village, napalm

Stuck to her dress like jelly,
Her hands reaching for the no one
Who waits in waves of heat before her.

So I can keep on living,
So I can stay here beside you,
I try to imagine she runs down the road and wings
Beat inside her until she rises
Above the stinking jungle and her pain
Eases, and your pain, and mine.

But the lie swings back again.
The lie works only as long as it takes to speak
And the girl runs only as far
As the napalm allows
Until her burning tendons and crackling
Muscles draw her up
Into that final position
Burning bodies so perfectly assume. Nothing
Can change that; she is burned behind my eyes
And not your good love and not the rain-swept air
And not the jungle green
Pasture unfolding before us can deny it.

Amnesia

If there was a world more disturbing than this
Where black clouds bowed down and swallowed you
    whole
And overgrown tropical plants
Rotted, effervescent in the muggy twilight, and
    monkeys
Screamed something
That came to sound like words to each other

Across the triple-canopy jungle you shared,
You don't remember it.

You tell yourself no and cry a thousand days.
You imagine that the crows calling autumn into place
Are your brothers and you could
If only the strength and will were there
Fly up to them to be black
And useful to the wind.

DEBORAH WOODARD

Tower

for David

In my dream you're wearing an old trenchcoat
identical to one my father donned at the last minute
for an ancient New York shot—
both of you know how to stand so quietly
another's heart is audible through a bleak rain.

Your dream hovers above us like the chopper
you called in for a napalmed Vietnamese girl.
The terrain it's crossing must be the mirror's flip side,
concealing villages and the new crop
of graves. There's a portrait of the wounded,
still unfinished. You want to complete it. I imagine
   you
attempting to turn the mirror right side up
and cutting yourself on a flawed edge.

Is there a way back from such thoughts
into the morning? The child leans his cheek
against the window of the outbound train,
and I think of how the ocean exchanges woes for
   seashells.
For a long time, a glimpse of you brought me to this
   water.
We held hands in the tower's shade, climbed to a
   dollhouse
room, a bed too small for sleep.

RAY A. YOUNG BEAR

Wadasa Nakamoon,
Vietnam Memorial

Last night when the yellow moon
of November broke through the last line
of turbulent Midwestern clouds,
a lone frog, the same one
who probably announced
the premature spring floods,
attempted to sing.
Veterans' Day, and it was
sore-throat weather.
In reality the invisible musician
reminded me of my own doubt.
The knowledge that my grandfathers
were singers as well as composers—
one of whom felt the simple utterance
of a vowel made for the start
of a melody—did not produce
the necessary memory or feeling
to make a Wadasa Nakamoon,
Veterans' Song.
All I could think of
was the absence of my name
on a distant black rock.
Without this monument
I felt I would not be here.
For a moment, I questioned
why I had to immerse myself
in country, controversy and guilt,

but I wanted to honor them.
Surely, the song they presently
listened to along with my grandfathers
was the ethereal kind which did not stop.

Notes on Contributors

MICHAEL ANANIA (b. 1939) Teaches English literature and creative writing at the University of Illinois at Chicago. Books include *New Poetry Anthology* (editor), *The Color of Dust* and *Riversongs* (poetry), and *The Red Menace* (fiction).

PHILIP APPLEMAN (b. 1926) U.S. Army Air Corps, 1944–45, aviation cadet and physical training instructor. Distinguished Professor of English at Indiana University. Author and editor of numerous books, the most recent of which are *Darwin* (editor), *Shame the Devil* (fiction), and *Darwin's Ark* (poetry).

JOHN BALABAN (b. 1943) Civilian alternative service as a conscientious objector, 1967–69. Service in Vietnam, 1967–69 and 69, primarily as field representative for the Committee of Responsibility to Save War-Injured Children. Returned to Vietnam in 1971, spending nearly a year traveling the countryside alone with a tape recorder while collecting the oral folk poems of Vietnamese farmers. Professor of English at Pennsylvania State University. Books include *After Our War* and *Blue Mountain* (poetry), *Ca Dao Vietnam* (translations of Vietnamese folk poetry), and *Coming Down Again* (fiction).

JAN BARRY (b. 1943) U.S. Army, 1962–65, weapons and infantry radio specialist. Service in Vietnam, 1962–63, 18th Avn. Co., U.S. Army Support Group. Resigned an appointment as a cadet at the U.S. Military Academy. Cofounder of Vietnam Veterans Against the War. Journalist and freelance writer. Coeditor of *Winning Hearts and Minds* and *Demilitarized Zones;* editor of *Peace Is Our Profession;* author of *War Baby* and *Veterans Day* (poetry).

R. L. BARTH (b. 1947) U.S. Marine Corps, 1966–69. Service in Vietnam, 1968–69, E. Co., 1st Recon. Bn. Teaches in the

English Department at Xavier University, Cincinnati, Ohio. Author of *Forced-Marching to the Styx* (poetry).

STEPHEN BERG (b. 1934) Writer, teacher, and editor. Cofounder of *The American Poetry Review*. Author of numerous books including *The Daughters, Grief, With Akhmatova at the Black Gates* and *In It*. Cotranslator of *Clouded Sky* by Miklos Radnati, and of *Oedipus the King*.

D. C. BERRY (b. 1942) U.S. Army Medical Service Corps, 1966–69. Service in Vietnam, 1967–68. Teaches at the Center for Writers, University of Southern Mississippi. Books include *Saigon Cemetery* and *Jawbone*.

ROBERT BLY (b. 1926) U.S. Navy, 1944–46. Poet, writer, translator, editor, and publisher. With David Ray, organized American Writers Against the Vietnam War, March 1966. Recently jailed in Minneapolis during an arms-race protest. Books include *Silence in the Snowy Fields, Sleepers Joining Hands*, and *The Man in the Black Coat Turns* (poetry), *The Kabir Book* (translations), *News of the Universe* (editor), and many others too numerous to list.

IGOR BOBROWSKY (b. 1946) U.S. Marine Corps, 1965–69, infantry. Service in Vietnam, 1967–68; D Co., 1st Bn., 5th Marines; CAP Delta One, 2nd CAG; Mobile CAP Team #1; 4th CAG. Researcher and writer for CBS TV Network News.

D. F. BROWN (b. 1948) U.S. Army, 1968–77, medic. Service in Vietnam, 1969–70, 1st/14th Inf. Bn., 4th Inf. Div. Working toward a master's degree in writing at San Francisco State University. Author of *Returning Fire*.

STEVEN FORD BROWN (b. 1952) Antiwar activist, 1969–71. General editor of the American Poets Profile Series and publisher of Ford-Brown & Co., Houston, Texas. Author of *Erotic Mask* and *The Thunder City Poems;* editor of *Contemporary Literature in Birmingham: An Anthology*.

THOMAS BRUSH (b. 1941) Teacher of English at Kent-Meridian High School, Kent, Washington. Author of *Opening Night*.

CHRISTOPHER BURSK (b. 1943) Teaches English at Bucks County Community College and Bucks County Prison. Author of three collections of poetry: *Standing Watch, Place of Residence,* and *Little Harbor.*

MARYLIN BUTLER (b. 1945) Writer. Author of the poetry collection *Half Past Sunset.* Wife of Vietnam veteran and novelist Robert Olen Butler.

JOSEPH CADY (b. 1938) Active in faculty peace work while teaching English at Columbia and Rutgers during the Vietnam War. Psychotherapist, poet, and scholar currently writing a book on 19th century gay male literature while on fellowship from the American Council of Learned Societies.

HAYDEN CARRUTH (b. 1921) U.S. Army Air Corps, 1942–45, cryptographer. Poet and writer. Author of twenty-five books including, most recently, *Asphalt Georgics* and *The Oldest Killed Lake in North America* (poetry), and *Effluences from the Sacred Caves* (criticism).

RON CARTER (b. 1941) U.S. Navy, 1964–67. Service in Vietnam, 1966, communications officer aboard *USS Bronstein* (DE–1037), South China Sea. Teaches English at Rappahannock Community College, Warsaw, Virginia.

RAY CATINA (b. 1948) U.S. Army infantry. Service in Vietnam, 1969–70. Occasionally tends bar in upstate New York.

HORACE COLEMAN (b. 1943) U.S. Air Force, 1965–70, air traffic controller. Service in Vietnam, 1967–68. Technical writer, Hewlett-Packard, San Diego Division. Author of *Between a Rock & a Hard Place.*

FRANK A. CROSS, JR. (b. 1945) U.S. Army draftee, 1969–70, light weapons infantryman. Service in Vietnam, 1969–70. Farms cotton, corn, and wheat near Chowchilla, California, in the San Joaquin Valley.

ROBERT DANA (b. 1929) U.S. Navy, 1946–48. Teaches in the English Department at Cornell College in Mt. Vernon, Iowa. Author of *Some Versions of Silence, The Power of the Invisible, In A Fugitive Season*, and *What the Stones Know*. Editor of *Against the Grain: Interviews with Maverick American Publishers*.

STEVE DENNING (b. 1947) U.S. Army, 1966–69, medic. Service in Vietnam, 1967–68, 25th Med. Recently returned from two years in Saudi Arabia where he served as materials manager for that country's first university-affiliated hospital.

W. D. EHRHART (b. 1948) U.S. Marine Corps, 1966–69. Service in Vietnam, 1967–68, Assistant Intelligence Chief, 1st Bn., 1st Marines. Writer, editor, and teacher. Books include *The Outer Banks & Other Poems* and *To Those Who Have Gone Home Tired: New & Selected Poems, Vietnam-Perkasie*, and *Passing Time* (nonfiction), *Demilitarized Zones* (coeditor), and *Those Who Were There* (contributing editor).

CHARLES FISHMAN (b. 1942) Director of the Visiting Writers Program, State University of New York at Farmingdale. Author of two poetry collections: *Warm-Blooded Animals* and *Mortal Companions*.

BRYAN ALEC FLOYD (b. 1940) U.S. Marine Corps, 1966–68. Teaches college on Long Island, New York. Author of two poetry collections: *The Long War Dead* and *Prayerfully Sinning*.

DAVID HALL (b. 1946) U.S. Army, 1966–69. Service in Vietnam, 1968–69, artillery forward observer, 9th Inf. Div. Author of *Werewolf and Other Poems* and the play *The Quality of Mercy*.

GUSTAV HASFORD (b. 1947) U.S. Marine Corps, 1966–68. Service in Vietnam, 1967–68, combat correspondent, Task Force X-Ray, 1st Mar. Div. Author of the novel *The Short-Timers*.

STEVE HASSETT (b. 1946) U.S. Army, 1966–68, infantryman and intelligence analyst. Service in Vietnam, 1966–67, Co. C, 1st Bn., 5th Cav., 1st Cav. Div. (Air Mobile). Later active with Vietnam Veterans Against the War. Staff attorney with Legal Services of Buffalo, a poverty law program, specializing in family law and veterans law.

SAMUEL HAZO (b. 1928) Former U.S. Marine. President and director of the International Poetry Forum. Most recent books include *The Wanton Summer Air* and *Thank A Bored Angel*.

GEORGE HITCHCOCK (b. 1914) Former editor of *Kayak*. Lecturer in Literature, University of California at Santa Cruz. Author of fifteen books, most recently *The Wounded Alphabet* (Poems 1953–83) and *Cloud-Taxis* (Poems 1984).

DANIEL HOFFMAN (b. 1923) U.S. Army Air Force, 1943–46. Director of the Writing Program at the University of Pennsylvania. Former poetry consultant to the Library of Congress. Author of numerous books of poetry and literary criticism including *The Center of Attention, Brotherly Love*, and *Poe Poe Poe Poe Poe Poe Poe*.

PETER HOLLENBECK (b. 1942) U.S. Army, 1967–69, Signal Corps. Poet and writer.

JOHN F. HOWE (b. 1947) U.S. Marine Corps, 1965–69. Service in Vietnam, 1966–67 and 1967–68. Chicago police officer assigned as a detective with the Gang Crimes Unit.

CHRISTOPHER HOWELL (b. 1945) U.S. Navy, 1968–70, journalist assigned mostly to carrier duty. Director of the Oregon Writers' Workshop and poetry editor for Lynx House Press. Books include *The Crime of Luck, Why Shouldn't I, Though Silences: The Ling Wei Texts*, and *Sea Change*.

DAVID HUDDLE (b. 1942) U.S. Army, 1964–67, military intelligence specialist. Service in Vietnam, 1966–67. Teaches literature and creative writing at the University of Vermont. Books include *A Dream with No Stump Roots in It, Paper Boy*, and *The Undesirable*.

ALLSTON JAMES (b. 1947) U.S. Army, 1969–71. Service in Vietnam, 1969, artillery forward observer. Teaches English and journalism at Monterey Peninsula College, California. Author of *Attic Light* (fiction) and *The Mile Away Contessa* (poetry).

HERBERT KROHN (b. 1938) U.S. Army, 1965–67, physician.

Service in Vietnam, 1966–67. Musician and member of Harvard Medical School faculty, specializing in emergency medicine.

YUSEF KOMUNYAKAA (b. 1947) U.S. Army, 1968–71, Information Specialist. Service in Vietnam, 1969–70, Americal Div. Teaches in the Poetry-in-the-Schools program and works as a producer at the Copacetic Cultural Center in New Orleans. Author of the poetry collections *Lost in the Bonewheel Factory, Copacetic,* and *I Apologize for the Eyes in My Head;* coeditor of *The International Poetry and Jazz Anthology.*

LUCY LAKIDES (b. 1954) Edited and published *Syncline,* 1977–84. Advertising account manager for *California Magazine.* Author of the play *Ghosts.*

JAMES LAUGHLIN (b. 1914) Poet, lecturer, and publisher of New Directions Books. Author of numerous books including *In Another Country* and *Stolen & Contaminated Poems.*

MCAVOY LAYNE (b. 1943) U.S. Marine Corps, 1966–67, infantryman. Service in Vietnam, 1966–77. Author of *How Audie Murphy Died in Vietnam.*

DENISE LEVERTOV (b. 1923) Poet and writer. Teaches English at Stanford University. Author of numerous books including *Collected Earlier Poems 1940–1960, Poems 1960–1967, Relearning the Alphabet,* and *Oblique Prayers.*

LOU LIPSITZ (b. 1938) Teaches political science at the University of North Carolina-Chapel Hill. Author of two volumes of poetry: *Cold Water* and *Reflections on Samson.*

DICK LOURIE (b. 1937) U.S. Army Reserve, 1961–66. Founder and editor of Hanging Loose Press. Author of the poetry collections *Anima, The Dream Telephone, Stumbling,* and *Letter to Answer.*

PAUL MARTIN (b. 1940) Teaches at Lehigh County Community College.

GERALD MCCARTHY (b. 1947) U.S. Marine Corps, 1965–68. Service in Vietnam, 1966–67. Author of the poetry collection *War Story.*

WALTER MCDONALD (b. 1934) U.S. Air Force, 1957–71, pilot and instructor. Service in Vietnam, 1969–70. Director of Creative Writing at Texas Tech University. Author of the poetry collections *Caliban in Blue, Burning the Fence, Anything, Anything, One Thing Leads to Another*, and *Working Against Time*. Coeditor of *A 'Catch-22' Casebook* and *Texas Stories & Poems*.

THOMAS MCGRATH (b. 1916) U.S. Army Air Force, 1942–45. Poet, writer and teacher. Author of numerous collections of poetry including *Letter to an Imaginary Friend, The Movie at the End of the World: Collected Poems, Passages Toward the Dark*, and *Echoes Inside the Labyrinth*.

RICHARD M. MISHLER (b. 1947) U.S. Army, 1967–70. Service in Vietnam, 1968–70. Freelance writer.

LARRY MOFFI (b. 1946) U.S. Army, 1969–71. Freelance writer and editor; associate director of the Cracker Jack Oldtimers Baseball Classic. Author of *A Simple Progression*.

JAMES MOORE (b. 1943) Draft resister, January to October 1970. Teaches at the Minneapolis College of Art and Design. Books include *The New Body, What the Bird Sees*, and *How We Missed Belgium* (with Deborah Keenan).

DAVID MURA (b. 1952) Taught special section of composition for Southeast Asian refugees (Vietnamese, Cambodian, Laotian, and Mung) at the University of Michigan, 1978–79. Teacher and writer. Living in Japan, 1985–86, while on U.S.-Japan Exchange Fellowship from NEA.

PERRY OLDHAM (b. 1943) U.S. Air Force, 1966–70. Service in Vietnam, 1969–70. English Department Chairperson, Casady School, Oklahoma City. Author of the poetry collection *Vinh Long*.

JOEL OPPENHEIMER (b. 1930) Poet, writer, and teacher. Author of numerous books, most recently *At Fifty, Just Friends/Friends & Lovers, Poetry, the Ecology of the Soul*, and *New Spaces*.

SIMON J. ORTIZ (b. 1941) U.S. Army, 1963–66. Service in the

Dominican Republic, 1965. Poet, writer, and performer. Author of *Going for the Rain, A Good Journey, From Sand Creek, Fight Back, Fightin', The People Shall Continue,* and *Howbah Indians.*

MARK OSAKI (b. 1952) Served in various civilian intelligence capacities in Southeast Asia. Writer and editor. Author of *Tradecraft.*

BASIL T. PAQUET (b. 1944) U.S. Army, 1966–68, medic. Service in Vietnam, 1967–68. Coeditor of *Winning Hearts and Minds* (poetry) and *Free Fire Zones* (short fiction).

ANTHONY PETROSKY (b. 1948) U.S. Army Reserve, 1970–75. Administrator for the Pittsburgh Public Schools and teacher at the University of Pittsburgh. Collections of poetry include *Jurgis Petrakas, The Look of Things, New Lives,* and *Waiting Out the Rain.*

JOHN CLARK PRATT (b. 1932) U.S. Air Force, 1954–74, pilot. Service in Vietnam and elsewhere in Southeast Asia, 1969–70. Teaches English at Colorado State University. Books include *The Laotian Fragments* (fiction), *Vietnam Voices* (compiler and editor), *The Meaning of Modern Poetry* and *John Steinbeck* (nonfiction), a critical edition of *One Flew Over the Cuckoo's Nest* (editor), and *George Eliot's "Middlemarch" Notebooks* (coeditor).

DON RECEVEUR (b. 1946) U.S. Army, 1969–71, medic. Service in Vietnam, 1970. Psychologist; deputy regional manager for Veterans Administration (Region V) Vet Center program offering readjustment counseling for Vietnam veterans.

DALE RITTERBUSCH (b. 1946) U.S. Army, 1966–69, infantry; operations and intelligence specialist. Service in Vietnam, 1968–69, Military Assistance Command—Thailand, Liaison Officer. Teaches creative writing and composition at Bowling Green State University, Ohio. Nonfiction editor of *The Mid-American Review.*

LARRY ROTTMANN (b. 1942) U.S. Army, 1965–68, infantry. Service in Vietnam, 1967–68. High school English teacher. Author of the novel *American Eagle;* coauthor (with Francie Rottmann) of the children's book *Eli's Pond;* coeditor of *Winning Hearts and Minds* (poetry) and *Free Fire Zones* (short fiction).

VERN RUTSALA (b. 1934) U.S. Army, 1956–58, draftee. Teaches English at Lewis & Clark College, Oregon. Author of *The Window, Laments, The Journey Begins, Paragraphs,* and *Walking Home from the Icehouse.*

JOHN C. SCHAFER (b. 1941) Served with International Voluntary Services in Vietnam, 1968–70; taught at University of Hué under the Fulbright Program, 1971–73. Professor of English at Humboldt State University, Arcata, California.

RICHARD SHELTON (b. 1933) U.S. Army, 1956–58. Teaches in the Creative Writing Program, Department of English, at the University of Arizona. Collections of poetry include *The Tattooed Desert, Of All the Dirty Words, Calendar, You Can't Have Everything, The Bus to Vera Cruz,* and *Selected Poems: 1969–81.*

JOSEPH A. SOLDATI (b. 1939) U.S. Army, 1962–64, intelligence. Service in Vietnam, 1962–64. Professor of English literature and writing at Western Oregon State College. Author of *Configurations of Faust: Three Studies in the Gothic (1798–1820).*

WILLIAM STAFFORD (b. 1914) Alternative service for conscientious objectors, 1942–46. Retired after teaching for over thirty years in various colleges; now writing full time. Author of numerous books including *Stories That Could Be True: New & Collected Poems, A Glass Face in the Rain* (poetry), and *Down in My Heart* (nonfiction).

MICHAEL STEPHENS (b. 1946) Teaches in the Writing Program at Columbia University. Author of *Still Life, Shipping Out, Circles End* and *Season at Coole* (fiction), *Alcohol Poems* and *Tangun Legend* (poetry), *Our Father* and *R&R* (plays), and *Translations* (English translations of Korean poetry).

FRANK STEWART (b. 1946) Left the U.S. during the Vietnam war. Writer. Author of the poetry collections *The Open Water* and *Flying the Red Eye.* Editor of *Poetry Hawaii, Talk Story: Hawaii's Local Writers,* and *InterChange.*

BILL TREMBLAY (b. 1940) Drafted August 1963 but did not serve due to President Kennedy's executive order exempting married men. Teaches creative writing at Colorado State University. Collections of poetry include *Crying in the Cheap Seats, The Anarchist Heart, Home Front,* and *Second Sun: New & Selected Poems.*

TOM WAYMAN (b. 1945) Member of Students for a Democratic Society at University of California at Irvine, 1966–68, and Colorado State University, 1968–69. Currently unemployed. Author of *Introducing Tom Wayman: Selected Poems 1973–1980, Going for Coffee: Poetry on the Job,* and *Counting the Hours: City Poems.*

RON WEBER (b. 1947) Freelance writer and editor.

BRUCE WEIGL (b. 1949) U.S. Army, 1967–70, communications. Service in Vietnam, 1967–68, 1st Air Cav. Professor of Creative Writing at Old Dominion University; associate editor of *Intervention* magazine. Author of four collections of poetry: *Executioner, A Sackful of Old Quarrels, A Romance,* and *The Monkey Wars.* Editor of *The Imagination As Glory: The Poetry of James Dickey* and *The Giver of Morning: The Poetry of Dave Smith.*

DEBORAH WOODARD (b. 1950) Teaches at California State University, Chico.

RAY A. YOUNG BEAR (b. 1950) Author of *Winter of the Salamander* (poetry) and editor of *Stories from the Woodland Region* (a collection of memoirs, translations, and traditional tribal stories).